T0078185

CALL ME BABAGBOSE

DAMO-FRIENDLY

CALL ME BABAGBOSE

The Comedy/The Movie

DAMOLA TAIWO

Call me Babagbose
The Comedy/The Movie

Copyright © 2013 by Damola Taiwo.

All rights reserved. No part of this book may be used or reproduced by any means, graphic, electronic, or mechanical, including photocopying, recording, taping or by any information storage retrieval system without the written permission of the author except in the case of brief quotations embodied in critical articles and reviews.

A SHORT COMEDY: STORIES & MOVIE SERIES

These stories featured in this book are not real.
These stories were created to entertain the readers and audiences.

BRING OUT YOUR LIGHTS, CAMERAS, AND EVENTS.THE MOVIE MUST BEGIN!

Author Damola Taiwo
Stories by Damola Taiwo
Directed by Damola Taiwo
Art by Damola Taiwo

iUniverse books may be ordered through booksellers or by contacting:

iUniverse
1663 Liberty Drive
Bloomington, IN 47403
www.iuniverse.com
1-800-Authors (1-800-288-4677)

Because of the dynamic nature of the Internet, any web addresses or links contained in this book may have changed since publication and may no longer be valid. The views expressed in this work are solely those of the author and do not necessarily reflect the views of the publisher, and the publisher hereby disclaims any responsibility for them.

Any people depicted in stock imagery provided by Thinkstock are models, and such images are being used for illustrative purposes only.
Certain stock imagery © Thinkstock.

ISBN: 978-1-4759-8678-5 (sc)
ISBN: 978-1-4759-8679-2 (e)

Print information available on the last page.

iUniverse rev. date: 06/17/2016

CONTENTS

CALL ME BABAGBOSE...THE JOURNEY CONTINUES...

A SHORT COMEDY: STORIES & MOVIE SERIES

Intro: Damola art studio 2013

THE LONELY AFRICAN LADY AND THE DRUMMER

THE LONELY AFRICAN LADY AND THE DRUMMER

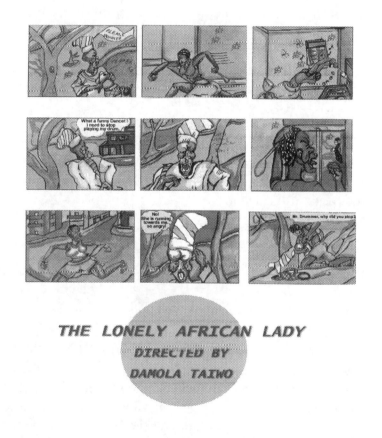

DAMOLA AFRICAN STORYBOARD COPYRIGHT RESERVED 2008. 2 OF 1   34c

A lonely lady was in search of a good husband. One afternoon, she was in her massive mansion. She was preparing her favorite rare delightful recipes. Certainly, rare dishes enriched with natural flavors. People who lived around her massive mansion believed she was very wealthy. She inherited her wealth from the rare delightful dishes. Twice a year, she prepared her rare delightful dishes.

Fortunately, people had the opportunity to taste her recipes. The invited guests had their mouths watered for more scoops of her dishes. They kept asking for more of her delightful dishes.

From experience, people claimed when you taste a teaspoon of her recipes, you won't stop asking for more of it. The rich guests seized every moment and tasted her delightful dishes. Indeed, the sweet sensation and aroma of her dishes.

The complimentary dishes consisted of corn, diced carrots, diced green peppers, diced red peppers, diced tomatoes, and rare spices. She slightly spiced her cooking with delightful herbs. The secrets of her cooking were the enriched natural spices. The prepared dishes had an authentic traditional rich taste.

On the outside atmospheric area, people walked by to have lunch and breaks from their work duties.

Some people walked by and attended family's gatherings.

It was one afternoon; she was lonely in her massive mansion. She was cooking in her kitchen. It was sunny on the outside of her mansion. A glimpse of glow was observed from the outside of her mansion. The people caught a glimpse of her face through the window of the mansion.

There was a drummer on the outside of the streets. He was nearly in his late 4o's. He was sitting beside the trees and closer to the woods. He was playing his traditional drum (ilu).

The drummer was a slim man and hard working. From the environment, people who walked by him enjoyed his music (drum). The lonely lady heard the sounds of the drum. She was stirring her cooking on the stove. She could hear the loud sound of the drum. She started dancing to the beats of the drum.

Accidentally, she cultivated the 'somersault' moves while dancing. Unfortunately, she broke the plates and glasses in her kitchen. Angrily, she stopped and glanced through her window.

She yelled, "That drummer must be responsible for breaking my furniture, plates, and my glasses."

The drummer saw a blurred vision of a lonely lady dancing through her window.

The drummer yelled, "She can't dance to my music for free, she must pay."

Jealously, he stopped playing his drum (music). Unpredictably, the lonely lady felt the silence from a drum on the outside of her mansion.

The lonely lady became very angry and yelled, "He is mine, forever."

She grabbed her shoes and ran out of her mansion. Furiously, the drummer saw the lonely lady running towards him. The crowd saw the lonely lady running towards them. Previously, she noticed the crowd were dancing towards the drummer's drum (music). Distantly, the crowd recognized the lonely lady as she approaches them.

The crowd ordered and persuaded the drummer to continue playing his drum (music).

Ignorantly, the drummer replied, "No." The crowd ran away from the drummer.

The drummer shouted, "Chickens, just a lady? You can't leave me alone over here."

The drummer yelled, "Let her face me, I'm not scared to face a lady."

In the neighborhood, people described the lonely lady as the richest and strongest lady in town.

In exaggeration, people assumed it was her special ingredients in her dishes that made her so strong.

Physically, she was built and hefty. The trees were frightened in the forest towards her arrival. The coconuts fell off from the trees. The birds on the trees flew away.

Surprisingly, the drummer asked, "Is it just me or was I dreaming previously?"

"I can't believe these trees, scared of just a lady, can someone grab me my bag and my drum?"

"I can't believe my eyes, No way! I have to run; I need to run out of here."

However, he was too late to run away. She grabbed the drummer with one hefty hand.

The lonely lady grabbed the drummer and slammed him towards the trees. For ten seconds, the drummer grew weakly and was speechless.

The lonely lady yelled, "You are my man, Forever."

Fragilely, the drummer replied, "You must be kidding me."

The drummer yelled at her, "You don't own me."

The lonely lady replied, "You broke my plates and glasses in my kitchen, you have to replace everything."

Politely, the drummer asked, "Mercy, Mercy, How is that possible?"

"I wasn't in your kitchen."

She replied, "Your music broke everything; I was dancing to your music."

The drummer asked, "How much?"

She replied, "60 goats and 60 chickens."

The drummer asked, "Where do you want me to get that kind of money from?"

The lonely lady replied, "Well, my plates and glasses were imported from the overseas."

The drummer replied, "A lonely unfortunate drummer like me, trying to survive."

The drummer replied, "Look at me, see how slim I am."

The drummer replied, "60 goats and 60 chickens will make me hunger-free."

Again, the drummer replied, "I need to gain some fat on me, look at me, I am a small man."

She replied, "You sure look like a skeleton."

"Your head is bigger than your body."

The drummer yelled, "At least, I'm good looking."

She glanced at the drummer's eyes.

The drummer yelled at her, "Never! Love, go away! Let me go."

She replied, "No! No!, You are mine, unless you pay for the damages."

She grabbed the drummer along with his drum to her mansion.

She fed the drummer with her delightful dishes. He played his drum and there were large variety of music for life. They compromised.

They lived forever happy. I was there, the writer, I saw it all! What a co-incidence!

Copyrighted materials-The lonely African Lady and the Drummer 2013

-The end-

Vocabulary: The drum was described as world's famous rare drum. The world's famous rare drum was called the 'ilu'. The 'ilu' was a drum used for entertaining the guests and the royal highness. The 'ilu' was originated from the great traditional native area. The 'ilu' had rhythm of sounds for dancing. It was played by using one's hands or drum sticks to beat the top surface of the drum. The top surface of the drum was made from real leather. The top leather was taken from the cow skin and the goat skin. The leather was dried on the outside atmospheric condition. The sunlight dries the leather whereby it creates interesting shades of white and brown. **Definition of Woods:** the trees and other plants in a large densely wood section of a place.

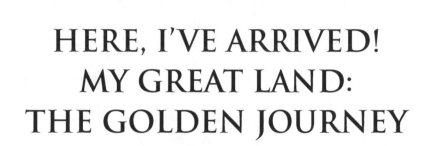

HERE, I'VE ARRIVED!
MY GREAT LAND:
THE GOLDEN JOURNEY

Here, I've Arrived! My Great Land!

Indeed! Beautiful atmospheric condition, I saw the herdsmen dragging the cows with a rope tied around the necks of the cows. There were goats and chickens within the beautiful environment. These animals were enjoying a life of freedom. However, I had my freedom of enjoying everything around me. I achieved pride within myself and accepted what was around me. Everything was a great journey for me to experience along the path. Romantically, I could smell the sweet atmospheric condition.

However, it helped me to get stronger to face anything that comes my way. From my observation, it was like being a great warrior.

The animals were moving around and eating whatever could be found on the streets (breeze of mind). And I loved it so much to experience everything.

Desperately, I glanced around and the animals seemed very healthy. However, I saw one of the animals running for its life (sensitivity).

I guessed these animals didn't want me to have them for lunch. Why couldn't I have these animals for lunch?

I yelled, "Hey! Chickens don't run from me, let me have you for my lunch, my belly is screaming hunger."

These animals wouldn't give me a chance. However, I couldn't blame the chickens and hens.

These were strong chickens and hens. These chickens had muscular features and I wondered if these animals were working out (gymnastics).

I wondered if it was possible for a chicken to lift a weight. Surprisingly, these chickens could break my face or slam my face towards a wall.

From my great experience, these animals were very sensitive. Would you blame these animals?

I thought hardly as I studied these animals,

"How did these chickens and hens have these unbelievable thoughts?"

However, some of these chickens and hens fed on dried foods; dried corns and nuts on the streets.

I wondered if these chickens and hens inherited some supplements (daily menu/ routine). However, that could be a source of daily nutrients (vitamins / proteins). Gratefully, I observed the beautiful sunshine and the shades of colors within the clouds.

I observed the pinkish, oranges, and blue schemes within the clouds. Romantically, I felt like hugging those clouds in the sky. And this was where I cherished the natural richness of my great land. The motherland is beautiful and great. Long live the atmosphere!

However, these clouds were up in the sky. But there was no way I could touch the clouds.

I thought for a while, "How was I supposed to climb the ladder to the sky?"

"Can anyone give me a suggestion?"

Definitely, a plane could have done the **'impossibility'** as I thought. It was amazing how the heavens created everything.

Amusedly, who else can create these beautiful clouds like that up in the sky? Artistically, we can draw and imitate those clouds in the skies. Definitely, Perfectionism was what we were looking for in life.

Let us get back to the movie. It was time to head back to the deep suburbs. Beautifully, I found colorful birds singing in the great deep suburban areas.

These beautiful birds were creative. These birds sang on the trees and within the skies. I realized the unpredictable theme songs of the birds (sweet melody). I wondered what the birds were singing and saying. I wished that I could sing like those flying colorful birds. I could described those songs as natural sounds of life. Creatively, I couldn't see the birds using any instruments for the sounds. There were beautiful sounds and I loved everything. I cherished the motherland and the atmospheric condition.

I was describing the atmospheric condition as not getting so cold as other great places. However, the cold weather was beautiful and creative too. I was able to create sculptures (ice).

In the deep forest and suburbs, I was told when trouble is heading the birds fly away and alert every creature.

There was a myth that when a lion is approaching the deep suburbs. The flying birds alert every creature in the deep suburbs.

The lion was described as the king of all animals (beast). I didn't want to face the lions.

Despite, lions were known to be wild and unfriendly in the deep suburbs. I respected the Lions and tiger's family. I couldn't imagine facing a lion. Let us just visualize a lion heading towards the back of us. Definitely, the first bite could be the buttocks.

I yelled at myself, "Aaaah! Not my buttocks, that wouldn't be nice."

However, I need to make a sign, "lions! stay away from me, go and find other flesh to consume."

"Not me! No way, I couldn't let a lion bite off my buttocks."

Fortunately, I need my full flesh covering my skeletal structure.

"How was I supposed to sit on a chair without a flesh on my buttocks?"

I wouldn't sit on a chair with bony buttocks on me. That wouldn't be nice and comfortable. My bones could pull apart one by one.

I yelled lonely, "Lions, Tigers, please stay away from me, go and feed on green plants; I can't be your supper."

In this great universe, I needed my buttocks to survive. I thanked the heavens for that perfect creation of my body.

Every part of the human body was created with perfectionism. I used the word 'perfectionism' to describe the daily duties of the human body.

Surprisingly, how many days did it take to create the human body? I couldn't estimate and I thanked the heavens.

Ouch! A mosquito bit me on my arm; that mosquito was telling me to keep my mouth shut.

I couldn't cheat nature and that shouldn't be a lesson.

Dear Readers,

Kindly pardon the appearance. My camera froze and I wondered what made it froze.

Could it be these mosquitoes? Maybe mosquitoes couldn't find peace too.

Maybe mosquitoes haven't had enough to eat too. I wasn't going to give up myself to the mosquitoes.

What kind of nutrients do these mosquitoes want? I was the cameraman and I was so confused.

Was it a source of '**animalv** . . . **tamin'** for these mosquitoes or what? I couldn't find that in my vocabulary.

I need to check another dictionary.

I ran out of roll of films in my camera. What an inexperienced cameraman we have here?

I yelled, "Nooo! I can't believe this; the mosquitoes ate the roll of films too."(Cameraman) As I was walking through the woods in the deep suburbs, I heard a crunchy sound underneath my feet (Sandals). I had the feeling I killed something underneath my feet.

I glanced underneath my feet and found out what had happened to my feet.

I saw a paralyzed soldier ant.

Accidentally, I realized, "What a life?

"I must have stepped on a soldier ant so hard and it crushed onto the ground."

Suddenly, one of the solider ants blew a trumpet.

Surprisingly, I saw heaps of soldier ants marching towards me.

These soldier ants had big heads and skinny body structures. I couldn't visualize an ant with a big head holding its skinny body.

The head structures were bouncing back and forth as these ants marched.

I thought, "Were these ants dancing or what? Was it a fashion show or parade?"

However, I could not figure it out.

Sensitively, I glanced and studied one of the ants. I noticed the head of the ant was still bouncing.

Was the head of the ant creating sounds of rhythms? It was like playing tennis game with a bat held at one's hand. The head of the ant was bouncing back and forth. In the human world, I couldn't have bounced my head like that of an ant's creativity. Honestly, my head could have fallen off towards the ground.

Was the ant showing off its buttocks, boutique, or what? I was not really paying attention to the ants. I needed more time to study the ants. However, it seemed as if it was a '**fashion show**' technique.

It was very hard for me to figure out the whole scenario.

May the heaven help us all in this great planet? I tried to rotate my video camera to get the entire scenes.

Amazing creatures, I guessed an ant must have informed the other soldier ants about the accident.

No way! I have to run and escape these soldier ants. From my observation, it felt like the ants were heading towards me.

Furiously, these ants were marching in lines to wage a war against me. Accidentally, I stepped on one of the soldier ants. How was I supposed to know that I stepped on one of the ants?

I ordered the ants, "Give me a break! Furious ants, I didn't mean to hurt one of your fellow ants."

The ants were not listening to me. No way! I have to run for my life.

Desperately, I asked, "Would somebody give me wings to fly?"

I wished I had wings on me to fly towards the beautiful skies.

However, there were so many unexpected situations which people go through in the deep suburbs

(earth).

These ants should give us some respect (human beings). Unpredictably, I felt a pain underneath the right toe of my feet.

Painfully, I screamed, "Uhhhh, my toes."

I glanced underneath my toes and found that an ant had bitten me.

Creatively, I yelled and asked, "Why me?"

I realized there was another ant in front of me within the forests.

Honestly, I was not expecting another ant aiming at me. I expected the ant to have fled from me.

Boldly, the ant stood up and showed off its smile.

Surprisingly, I yelled, "Was this ant showing off its great smile or what?"

Well, I have great smile to show the world too. I felt like kicking the ant out of my face.

I requested, "Would someone give me a hand to kick this ant out of my face?"

Creatively, it seemed as if the ant was giving me a sign language with its body.

I realized an ant was asking me if I wanted more bites. Mercy! I wasn't a candy bar to be bitten on.

I yelled at the ant, "No way! Not in my face, don't give me orders?"

Dear readers and audiences,

"A brother needs a help over here, come and rescue me."

This tiny ant could not be aiming at my body. Despite, there are so many plants to feed on as breakfasts, lunches, and suppers. Why could these ants want me as a meal? How much can these ants consume?

"According to the size of an ant, how many quantity of food can an ant eat in this big universe?"

This tiny ant could not be controlling me in this territory.

"Get me a whip."

"Take a look at my body, not enough flesh covering my bones."

"How many bites can my body take?"

"Physically, I was not a big man."

"This tiny ant doesn't care and wants to bite every piece of me."

I yelled, "Enough of my words of speculations."

"It seemed like everywhere around me was getting a little bit darken (atmosphere)."

I looked around me and there were huge numbers of ants.

Jeeezzz! I realized the ants had increased in numbers. How was I supposed to escape these ants?

Definitely, these ants could finish me up if I couldn't come up with a great idea.

I yelled at the ants, "Peace! Mercy! Peace! Human being is going down."

Surprisingly, I noticed a captain within the woods. I figured that was the captain of the ants.

From my observation, the captain had the biggest head with a smaller body structure. However, the captain of the ants looked so mean. Honestly, this was the ugliest ant which I have encountered in my life. Cowardly, I didn't want to face the captain of the ants. This could be the worst scenario that I have ever experienced in my life.

Defensively, I asked, "Would someone get me a dark shade? I need to close my eyes."

I realized that I had a match stick in my pocket. I forgot to tell you all that I was a great cigar smoker.

However, this could not be happening. Competitively, a captain gave out an order towards its fellow ants.

From my observation, I realized the ants had moved closer to me. And I had to find ways of escaping these ants.

I brought out my match stick and yelled, "Caution, Don't come closer; I would light this matchstick."

The soldier ants didn't believe me. I lit a matchstick and threw it at the dried leaves (bushes).

The dried leaves caught fire. Cowardly, the soldier ants moved backwards.

From my observation, I realized the match stick and the burning leaves scared the soldier ants away.

I thought the battle was over. One of the soldier ants flew towards me. I lit the match stick and threw it at the soldier ants.

Painfully, a soldier ant screamed, "My buttocks are on fire."

I thought for a second and asked,

"Did I hear an ant screaming something? Whose buttocks were on fire?"

I wouldn't care if the buttocks were crispy burnt (dark). These ants should just stay away from my sight.

This was not a joke for me playing with the match sticks and fire. I could get burnt by the presence of the fire. Defensively, it was not funny and I was watching out for my buttocks too.

I warned and ordered the soldier ants to leave at once. I thought I won the battle against the soldier ants.

All of the sudden, the soldier ants flew over me. Defensively, I had an extra fuel container in my pocket. I sprinkled it on the dried leaves around me. I lit the match stick and the fire went emblazed. Desperately, I glanced at the tall trees around me. I jumped on the ropes which were covering the trees. I climbed upwards and moved towards the top of a tree.

I realized that the captain of the ants was torn into pieces on the ground.

Happily, I yelled at the fallen ants,

"That's what you get from being creative with the papa of the forest."

"Look at me; I am the papa of the forest."

"Nobody plays with the papa of the forest, I own this place."

The soldier ants ran away and some of the soldier ants fell apart. I swung along the ropes of the tall trees to escape the endangered species.

-The End-

THE HUNGRY MOSQUITOES PT.1

Creatively, it was 5am in the morning, and I was dreaming about the universe. However, I saw the universe occupied with the insects and mosquitoes.And the insects didn't want to leave the human beings alone. Inspiring, I had great people and warriors in my dreams. My fact and theory was that: No matter where you go in the world, the insects and animals are always present in life. Suddenly, my ears itched and I woke up and stepped into the bathroom.

Surprisingly, I thought, "Who was singing those words into my ears?"

I washed my face and felt an itch at the upper section of my right arm. I had a feeling it must have been those unexpected guests. Those unexpected guests never had enough in life. What else do they want?

I was referring to the mosquitoes as the unexpected guests. I had the feeling the mosquitoes had bitten me. I glanced at the wall clock and I realized it was my day off from my work duties.

Angrily, I headed back to my bed and slept off. I heard a buzzing and creative sound within my ears.

Certainly, there were two noisy mosquitoes. It sounded as if these mosquitoes were playing drums within my ears. I felt it was very instrumental for these animals to invade my privacy.

From my observation, it sounded like an instrumental sound. It was as if the mosquitoes had drumming sticks to create that instrumental sound. Maybe I should start dancing to the sound and scare the mosquitoes away.

I yelled at the mosquitoes, "Mercy! Please, mercy! Leave! Let me sleep."

I yelled again, "mosquitoes, kindly mind your business."

However, these mosquitoes were not willing to stay way from human beings.

Dear readers, I have **one** or **two** questions to ask you all.

"Did the mosquitoes create a set up of business in the past?"

Or

"Was it a setup of biting human beings?"

Despite, the heavens created these enriched plants to feed on in this great universe. These mosquitoes preferred to bite on human beings. I realized wherever you go in this entire globe that the animal invades one's privacy. These animals were present within the scenes. I wondered who invited these animals.

Desperately, I ordered and cried out to the universe, "Would someone get me a broom?"

From observation, people called me a '**crying baby**'. I wasn't only a '**crying baby**' as I guessed in all my life. However, there wasn't any feeding bottle in my mouth. I was confused by that nick name.

And unpredictably, I asked the universe, "Who sent these mosquitoes?"

These mosquitoes were willing to bite me for breakfast, lunch, supper, and snack time.

Creatively, I yelled and asked, "Who sent these mosquitoes?"

I needed a sweeping broom. I stood up and picked up my sweeping broom. I wanted to smack and whip the life out of these creative mosquitoes. I couldn't bear any more of these creative works from these mosquitoes. These mosquitoes were invading my privacy. Creatively, I made my own code of conduct.

Unfortunately, I lost and I could not aim at these mosquitoes. The problem was that I was not aiming the broom at the right directions. The mosquitoes managed to bite me on my feet, my cheek, and my arm. It must have been a creative and juicy bite for these mosquitoes.

I thought, "**Jeeeez**! Double punishment for my body."

Dear readers, at the beginning of my movie, I managed to introduce you to my fearless buddies.

These mosquitoes were the fearless buddies which I was referring to you all.

Unfortunately, I couldn't have any other nick names to give these mosquitoes.

"Would any one give me a suggestion on how to heal these sore wounds?"

Recklessly, I shouldn't have scratched my arm so hard.

Painfully, my arm and cheeks were swollen and I should have stopped chasing those mosquitoes.

My dear readers,

"Ouch . . .! Why didn't I listen to my conscience?"

Surprisingly, these mosquitoes were very fast and I could see the sharp teeth through my magnifier.

Angrily, I asked, "Who sent these fearless butt teeth mosquitoes?"

Fortunately, I overheard the mosquitoes saying a word towards my ears.

"Did I hear the mosquitoes screaming a word like '**yummy**'?"

Precisely, I have to check my dictionary or vocabulary.

Despite, I wasn't designed as a meal, plate, or dish for these mosquitoes.

Painfully, I needed to stop scratching my arm, feet, and my cheeks.

At the end of the day, I was running around to stay away from the mosquitoes.

Who would believe me that I felt sick?

These fearless mosquitoes bit me so nicely. Who was going to judge these mosquitoes?

These mosquitoes enjoyed every piece of me (biting). My mouth was sour and bitter. I couldn't eat any food to make me feel better that day. From my observation, I guessed that every bitten part tasted so deliciously to the mosquitoes. Definitely, that wasn't funny to me.

How many more bites can my body take?

My body felt so weak. I was thinking if these mosquitoes caused my sickness. I couldn't figure it out and I was so tired. Desperately, I sent for my house maid. She purchased the dried tea leaf remedy from the traditional pharmacy. She gave me the curable medicine for my sickness.

She prepared me some boiled bitter leaves (high quality unprocessed tea). The boiled leaf tea was the traditional way of healing my sickness. I took some sips from the leaf tea. It felt so good and healthy.

Gladly, I yelled, "Mercy! Mercy! Whew." I slept like a baby in the crib.

Few hours later, I felt a slight improvement from my sickness. I didn't have to go to the clinic. This tea was obtained and found from my great land. I cherished my tea more than anything else. My health was my main concern. I found that good health was more valuable in life. When one has good health it brings happiness. However, it was mother nature. I observed from its rich nutrients.

Despite, I don't like injections. I was scared of the big needle heading to my buttocks.

I yelled, "No way! Not my tiny buttocks."

Despite, I was fragile and slim. How many needles can my body take as a treatment?

I didn't want to see every bone of my body to break into pieces.

Loudly, I yelled at housemaid in my compound, "Give me my food and medication."

From my observation, I realized the clinic and hospital bills could be very expensive. I realized good health brings more happiness than luxury. However, good health was more important than luxury in life.

Despite, the clinic and the hospital consisted of one of the best treatments for the patients.

Despite, one could head to the deep suburbs and get these great plants to heal sickness (herbs).

However, I had pride within the great environment of my culture and which I was living.

I thanked the heavens for the natural medications.

-The end-

THE HUNGRY MOSQUITOES PT.2 / THE CLUB SCENE: OVERSEAS

4. Hungry Mosquitoes *Pt.2 / The Club Scene: Overseas*

Suddenly, the wall clock of my room buzzed. It was morning and I was fully recovered from my sickness. A mail lady was delivering envelopes to every home within the neighborhood. Surprisingly, I wasn't expecting any mail at all. Despite, all my friends have relocated to the overseas to study. I was the only one in the deep suburbs. Pleasantly, I love my home sweet home towards any conditions (atmosphere).

Career wisely; I was doing well with my daily work. The manufacturing and agricultural businesses were noted to be a great ambition. I planted corn, cassava, yam, and coffee nuts for the food and industries.

One afternoon, a mail lady arrived and handed me so many addressed letters. I had the feeling it was good news and nothing bad.

Desperately, I opened one of my letters and noticed a foreign stamp. Joyfully, I realized one of my friends sent me an invitation letter with an important document. I was excited about everything from the letter.

Readers and audiences, I realized it was time for me to visit the overseas. My Prayers were answered from the heavens and I was amazed.

Desperately, I brought out my travel suit case and threw some clothes into it.

It was time for me to get prepared and leave the country. Precisely, I planned on leaving the next day. Majestically, I walked to my bed and started munching kola nuts (obi) as a dessert.

Obi was believed to be an unprocessed rare traditional nut from my great land. It was a sour—bitter nut which helped to improve one's health. It has so many nutrients to improve the performance of the human body. I contacted my local taxi cab services to take me to the airport. I didn't want to miss my flight to the overseas. Thank goodness, the taxi driver arrived on time to pick me up. As I was about to head to the taxi cab, I waived a 'good bye' to my great housemaid. I abandoned my occupational livestock.

The goats, cows, and chickens were my occupational livestock in my surroundings (occupation; pets: livestock).

Those were my occupational livestock duties which I mentioned to you all.

My fearless guests were the mosquitoes, bees, and the other soldier ants. Definitely, my fearless guests would miss me for breakfasts, lunches, and suppers.

Definitely, it was time for me to run from these fearless guests. I didn't want my fearless guests to finish me all. How much can I offer? In fact, wherever you go in this planet; the insects, spiders, and other animals were present.

Physically, I was small and I had nothing to offer these fearless guests (insects/mosquitoes).

All I could offer was '**smacking the smoke**' out of them. I succeeded with the help of my sweeping broom.

My fearless guests didn't want to listen to me. I realized that these fearless guests were willing to bite me and finish me up (body).

I asked, "Was I designed as a meal for the mosquitoes at the entire day?"

Mockingly, I yelled at my hungry guests, "Go and feed on the plants, not human beings."

I yelled at the taxi driver, "Enough of my words of speculations and take me to the airport."

The taxi driver was driving at full speed on the rocky roads.

Several times, I knocked and bumped my head at the ceiling of the taxi cab.

I yelled at the taxi driver, "Is this world war 1 or world war 2?"

Politely, I begged the taxi driver and asked him to drive carefully.

The taxi driver slowed down. However, the taxi driver was a great driver and he didn't want me to miss my flight.

Unfortunately, something stopped at the front of the taxi cab. There were two goats standing in front of the taxi cab.

The driver yelled at me, "Animals are smiling at each other."

I asked the driver, "What do you mean by saying; animals are smiling at each other?"

The driver replied, "Appointments and gatherings."

Angrily, I asked the driver, "What are these animals doing?

Repeatedly, he replied, "There are two goats in front of my taxi cab making up appointments."

I could not understand what the driver was telling me. I was so furious and I felt like getting off the taxi cab.

I asked the driver why the two goats were making up for each other. I raised my eyes up towards the front windshield of the taxi cab. I realized there was a camel in the midst of two goats. There were two goats standing together. However, I couldn't believe my eyes and this couldn't be real at all.

Unbelievably, this could not be happening when I was about to travel out of the country.

Furiously, I had a harsh reaction towards these animals.

"Were the two goats having a ceremony or what?" I couldn't believe my eyes.

I screamed, "Illusions, please, wipe it out of my sight."

"Do animals perform ceremony too or something? Was I dreaming or what?"

I thought appointments were designed for human beings alone.

From the whole scenario, I observed the animal kingdom was getting in the way.

I yelled at the taxi driver, "Not in my face, drive off, I can't miss my flight."

Surprisingly, I thought, "This could not be happening and I didn't want to miss my flight to the overseas."

I persuaded the driver, "we could have these goats for lunch (Grill), what do you think Mr. Driver?"

The driver answered, "There wouldn't be any barbeque sauce to spice it up."

Hurriedly, I thought, "I don't have time for this interruption."

I ordered the driver, "Please drive your car."

The taxi driver yelled at me, "Don't interrupt the appointment of these animals."

I yelled at the taxi driver, "rubbish."

Again, I yelled at the taxi driver, "I don't have time for these unreal appointments of these animals."

I yelled again at the taxi driver, "These animals need some serious creative smacking on the head."

"Drive your taxicab; I can't afford to miss my flight."

The driver yelled again, "I can't drive across these animals and every pathway of the road was blocked."

The taxi driver yelled back, "Give them time to finish up the meeting."

I yelled again at the taxi driver, "Finish what, meetings, appointments or what? I need my whip."

I walked out of the taxi cab and faced the goats. I gnashed my teeth and raised my fist towards the goats. Cowardly, I ran back into the taxi cab. I realized the goats were hefty and muscular (big horns). Were the goats working out? I couldn't see any weight lifting.

Definitely, I would need a helmet to protect my face and body. I needed my face and my teeth.

I wouldn't want to face these goats. Where did that muscular description come from?

I asked the taxi driver, "Was that a goat or a cow. which I saw in seconds? The driver was speechless.

Suddenly, the goats moved to the front section of the taxi cab. The goats moved backwards and faced the front section of the taxis cab.

Unbelievably, the two goats yelled back, "Take this and catch this."

The front windshield of the taxi cab was covered with goat wastes and dumps.

Surprisingly, I was speechless for two seconds.

However, I managed to ask myself, "What the he . . . . k? Would a goat say something like that?"

Annoyingly, I yelled at the goats, you **'voo . . .do . . .o'** goat heads! Get a cave, or something."

The taxi driver yelled at me,

"See what you have done to my precious taxi cab, I warned you not to interrupt those goats,"

"You wouldn't listen to me, why did you call the goats . . . **'voo . . .do . . .o'** goat heads?"

Desperately, the taxi driver managed to drop me at me airport.

The taxi driver yelled at me, "Don't you ride my car again." Angrily, the taxi driver drove away.

I couldn't blame the taxi driver for his anger towards me. I realized with all the problems that I have caused him with those goats. I paid the taxi driver all the damages which I caused him.

I felt so sad for the taxi driver. I didn't want to miss my flight to the overseas.

Honestly, it was once in a life time opportunity to travel to other beautiful places.

I wondered why the taxi driver took the rough way; he should have taken the expressway to the airport.

My clothes were stained and smelled like goat and I couldn't figure it out. Why me? I wish I could use the washroom of the airport. I needed a quick bath and where can I find one?

Maybe it wasn't that bad as I thought. However, these goats stained my outfit and was it cologne?

Finally, I had 35 minutes to board my plane to the overseas.

Unexpectedly, the crowd yelled at me, "What is that smell? Smells like 'dumps'"

I thought, "What could I say? It could be cologne and it must be my imagination."

I yelled back at them, "Must be you all, not me, stay away from me."

I kept a distance away from the crowd.

Angrily, I thought, "Those goats shouldn't have sprayed that creative cologne dumps."

Definitely, the taxi cab's windshield was covered with dumps and it wasn't funny. The driver should take his cab to the car wash.

However, I should have taught those two goats a lesson.

Maybe, I should have given those goats serious smacking of life. Being human, those goats should have given me some respect. I couldn't have enough time to give those goats serious smacking of life. These animals were always around me. I could just have these goats for supper (grilled / fried).

Unfortunately, I ran out of time. Definitely, this wasn't funny at all. Finally, the ticket agent issued my boarding ticket. I checked in my suitcases. I carried my hand luggage with me on the plane.

I had some sandwiches and kola nuts in my hand luggage.

However, I forgot my roasted plantains and roasted peanuts at home (groundnuts).

Marvelously, I carried my hand luggage with me to my seat on the plane.

I made it to the plane just at the right time.

Who would believe me? This would be my first time getting on the plane. I didn't know how to fasten my belt as illustrated by the flight attendant. Fortunately, I was educated in other areas, but I wasn't taught enough about planes. However, I was nervous, because modern technology had gone so advanced. My complimentary gesture towards the geniuses, scientists, and engineers of the universe.

The plane attendant showed me how to fasten my belt.

Joyfully, I wondered what was new on the agenda.

I brought out my sandwiches from my small hand luggage. Surprisingly, I found a tooth shaped holes in my sandwiches. Why me? I couldn't believe my eyes. It seemed as if the ants took some bites from my sandwiches. The ants must be hungry or something.

I thought, "May the heaven help us all, can I hear an '**ame . . . . n'** from anyone?"

I asked deeply, 'Was that a work of art' on my sandwiches?" I must be dreaming. However, I was not happy, but my mind kept saying these words, "Don't worry" Be V.I.P,"

I screamed, "**Nooooooo!** Not my sandwich, give me a break."

Surprisingly, the lady beside me glanced at me and asked, are you talking with yourself?"

I replied her, "The slices of my sandwiches have been shaped like the art of an ant."

"How I wished I had a sweeping broom to smack those ants."

I thought, "How was I supposed to eat these sandwiches?" I just couldn't eat my sandwiches.

Politely, I handed my sandwiches to a flight attendant.

Respectfully, I begged her to toss it into the trash compartment. Oh gracious, the plane was about to take off to the sky. I was scared of heights.

My stomach started making noise on the plane.

Silently, I asked my self, "Was I hungry or what?" I tried so hard to hold my stomach. It was kicking me so hard.

Even the lady next to my seat heard the loud noise from my stomach.

She yelled at me angrily, "That was disgusting."

I replied to her and said, "Thank you, it's my pleasure." And I was hoping my stomach would stop making that noise.

From my observation, it felt like my stomach was speaking a language.

Whacka! whacka! I heard that noise coming from my stomach.

I whispered, "What the **Bunch**? What does '**Whacka! whacka!**' Mean?"

"I hope my stomach won't '**whacka! Whacka'** my face?"

Maybe I should get a dictionary and find the meaning of that strange word (**whacka! Whacka!**).

I whispered within, "Was that creative? Excuse my language."

The lady next to my seat thought I passed out something into the air. She held her nose very tight.

And she snapped, "**Jeeez**! What kind of human being are you? Take it to the washroom."

I glanced at her and replied, "You must be kidding me."

I felt guilty about the whole scenario and it was my stomach that caused everything.

This stomach of mine knows how to disgrace me in the presence of people.

Vocabulary: As reference

whack-a-mole - definition of whack-a-mole in English from Dictionary

1 (Whac-a-Mole) A game in an amusement arcade in which ... you are near a amusement park, go in and play around of *whack-a-mole*.

I thought for a while, "How could I keep it shut? Any suggestions should be welcomed."

Quietly, I held my stomach very tight and I couldn't control it.

Politely, I managed to get back to the beautiful lady beside me; I extended my apology to her.

She switched on her head phones and minded her business. I wondered what type of language my stomach was speaking.

Definitely, it must be screaming '**hunger, hunger, and hunger**!'

Creatively, I pushed forward and punched my stomach with my fist. It felt like experimenting in science. Finally, my stomach stopped making that sound of breeze. Maybe, my stomach tried to lecture me how the stomach works in life. The beautiful lady beside me was intimated towards what I did. Surprisingly, I tried to be creative by keeping my stomach quiet within the time ratio. I couldn't cheat nature. Maybe nature couldn't cheat my stomach (sounds of melody).

I was glad my stomach stopped and that was a great relief. However, it felt so good.

The flight attendant walked towards us.

And she asked politely, "Is everything okay?"

I glanced at her and replied, "There was a noise coming from a passenger's stomach on the plane and it was knocking my face up and down."

"And I was wondering where that noise was coming from."

The flight attendant was speechless. The flight attendant deodorized the atmospheric condition of the plane.

"Wow!" I thought. Pleasantly, I love that sweet aroma of that deodorizer.

Dear readers and audiences,

What was I supposed to say? I couldn't tell the flight attendant that it was my stomach. I couldn't cheat nature. She was so pretty and it would be embarrassing if I told her that I was responsible for everything.

Delightfully, the flight attendants served us lunch from the menu. The served dish was so delicious that I stuck my fingers into my mouth and licked them. I was so filled up that I had to burp out so loudly.

Respectfully, I whispered, "Excuse me."

The lady beside me yelled again, "That was disgusting, don't you have manners?"

I needed a tooth pick for my teeth. I realized there was a piece of food and it was stuck within my teeth.

I couldn't see that piece of food within my teeth. I felt something stuck between my teeth and gum.

I needed a mirror to view that stuff stuck within my teeth. I asked the lady beside me if she could see anything stuck in my teeth.

She snapped, "Oh! **Jeeez!** I am not your dentist or your mama, take it to the washroom."

I thought within, "This lady must be one lonely person."

19

Who could ever believe such a beautiful lady could talk to me like this? Indeed, I felt embarrassed by her reaction towards me on the plane.

Successfully, my plane arrived at my final destination to the overseas. My friends were waiting for me at the arrival section of the airport. Amazingly, I found my friends at the arrival section of the airport.

Happily, we embraced each other as I entered my friend's vehicle. They carried my luggage and took me to the hotel room. The hotel rooms were noted to be the best which I admired so much in the world.

Definitely, my friends owned the company shares of the hotel business in town. Hotel business is a good investment in town. Honestly, people would always buy and eat food. Everyone needs food to survive.

I checked in to the hotel room and unpacked my clothes from my luggage. I had my dinner and slept off in my bed for a whole day. Finally, it was morning at 7am on the clock. The phone rang and I picked it up. It was the hotel attendant complimenting me on a free breakfast menu. I requested for healthy cereal and a cup of coffee. I jumped out from my bed and went to the washroom (bathroom). I brushed my teeth and took a quick bath. This was quite different from my home town. Fortunately, there were elegant hotels in this lovely planet. However, I never had time to visit these hotels in my home town.

I was so busy with my manufacturing business and agricultural business. However, traveling to the overseas gave me relaxation and relief from my hard work. Once in a life time, it is good to treat yourself.

Despite, I traded my enriched crops as an occupation within the beautiful living of my golden home town.

Enough of my words of speculations! Let us talk about the overseas.

The hotel attendant brought my breakfast to my room and served me a cup of coffee.

The phone rang and I picked it up. My friends informed me that we were going to the night club tonight.

They told me the taxi driver was heading to pick me up. I put on my traditional outfit and the head gear.

I thought it was a traditional gathering party of celebration.

The hotel passengers and visitors glanced at my traditional outfit. They admired my traditional outfit and it was a rare piece.

I ignored them and entered the reserved taxi cab. I arrived at the night club and jumped out of the taxi cab.

The night club security guard yelled at me, "What a great outfit? This is not a king's and queen's castle." Pardon me! My royal highest of all."

The security guard yelled again, "What an expensive rare traditional outfit you have here, who sent you?"

I begged the security guard to let me into the night club.

The security guard accepted me into the night club. I saw my friends and they greeted me. They admitted it was their faults by not telling me the dress code to the night club.

My friends embraced me and told me to move freely in the night club. I saw the bar section. There were many beautiful ladies at the bar section. They were laughing and enjoying their drinks over there.

I walked to the bar section, I ordered for non-alcoholic drink. The ladies at the bar stared at me as if I was a teenager. I guessed they thought I was scared to drink alcohol.

I felt shy and embarrassed by the way they stared at me. I meant I didn't like alcoholic drinks.

I cancelled my order and asked the bar attendant to serve me another drink.

The bar attendant said," Don't worry be 'V.I.P'."

One of the ladies loved my native accent. She said my native accent was very unique.

She discussed about how beautiful Africa was in the pictures. Someday, she said she would love to visit the motherland.

And I admired her complimentary gesture.

I thought quietly,

"My home Sweet home, I cherish you, my home."

She made me feel like crying towards her complimentary gesture.

Let us go back to my glass of drink; I couldn't finish it all and it was too strong.

One of the ladies at the bar section yelled, "Drink on my man, that's what I call a man."

Several times, I coughed and felt strong enough to dance on the floor. I had enough and I stood up from my seat. I walked towards the dance floor of the night club.

There were so many people dancing with each other on the dance floor.

I was so shy and I didn't know which one of the ladies to dance with on the dance floor. I kept on dancing my head off on the dance floor. The crowd glanced at my traditional outfit. The ladies loved my outfit. One of the ladies touched my outfit. I was humble and shy.

One of the ladies at the night club stared at me. Was she flirting with me? I couldn't tell at all. She was admiring my traditional outfit and I could see it in her beautiful eyes.

One of the dancers yelled, "Holy mercury."

I yelled back to the dancers, "What mercury, space or what?"

I yelled back again, "my people, there is no mercury fish over here, dance your heads off."

Later, I ignored them and kept dancing my heads off on the dance floor. I realized that I was making myself happy with the perfect ladies. However, I was enjoying myself which counts in life. Happiness counts in life. I found out without happiness, Life can be meaningless.

My eyes were closed while I was dancing at the night club.

However, I wasn't familiar with the dark lights at the night club. Accidentally, I punched people's faces with my fist. I meant, it felt like punching bags and my eyes were closed (shy). Thoughtfully, it felt like the stage was dancing too (Wall vibrating).

I kicked noses, feet, teeth, and lips. I kicked the crowd off from the dance floor.

I heard someone yelled, "My feet, my nose, my back, and my head."

The crowd yelled, "Man, get off the dance floor." I thought for a while, they should be glad I was dancing on the stage with the great ladies. 'Go for the golden cup."

The crowed yelled again, "What kind of dance was that?"

The security guard yelled, "My great prince, brother! No 'Exotic Fast dance' here on the floor."

I yelled back at the security guard, "This is not an 'Exotic Fast dance', it's a traditional dance."

I yelled back at the security guard, "I'm not a prince; I'm just a regular person."

The security guard yelled again, "I shouldn't have let you into this night club."

Immediately, I feared and started sweating as if I was going to fall apart. I meant the security guard was so built and tall. There was no way I could face him.

The security guard carried me and slammed me on the ground.

Unfortunately, my friends left the night club with their girlfriends before the incident.

There wasn't anybody in the night club to help me. The security guard held my neck. I decided to kick him at his lower section. Excuse my language. What could I have done to escape this tough situation?

The security guard yelled, "How could you kick that place?"

I felt so sad and I had to kick him there with my feet to release me.

The security guard fell weak on the floor.

The security guard yelled, "My people get him."

Sadly, I asked, "How was I supposed to know that I kicked noses, feet, and heads of the dancers?"

Accidentally, I must have broken their noses, feet, and teeth. That could be very expensive to replace in a life time.

Definitely, it was so dark and I couldn't see anything. I was scared of dark shaded lights.

However, I heard all kinds of songs which I had to balance it with my traditional dance moves.

I didn't know how to dance these great underground dance songs and other great remixes. I admired **electronic dance** music. Creatively, I wondered how these great songs were made in this great universe.

The great geniuses and masters created these great songs.

From my observation, these were songs made to be the greatest of all times.

Creatively, I honored these great songs of all times.

I yelled at the crowd, "Would somebody teach me how to dance these greatest songs of all times?"

"A Brother needs help over here like me."

The crowd yelled, "Get him."

It was embarrassing what I did on the dance floor. I kicked noses, heads, backbones, and feet of the people on the dance floor. I thought they forgave me. Desperately, I had to escape this night club.

I noticed all the troubles that I have caused them at the night club. However, it was time for me to run from this place. I ran to the washroom in the night club. I flipped the small window and flew through it.

Desperately, I ran outside towards a taxi cab and he drove me away.

I was glad that I escaped the night club's scene.

"Can you all imagine how many fists and hands would get on me?"

Dear readers and audiences,

From my observation, I was thinking towards myself, "Why did I do that? What made me to do it?"

"Well, ladies! This is my life, I am here for life, Babagbose for life, go for the gold,"

"May the heavens forgive me?"

"Take a look at me; I was a small person in nature.

I'm talking about serious smacking of Life (creative works of life)."

"No way, not my body, I had to run out of here."

-The end-

PINK LADY BUG: CHERISH HER WORLD: THE ANIMAL KINGDOM

5. The Pink lady Bug: Cherish Her World

Damola art sketch studio 2013

It was morning and I was singing towards the beauty of pink lady bug within her territory.

"O Beautiful! Beautiful! Pink lady bug! How beautiful your kingdom is towards my sight."

There were colorful butterflies flying within her precious garden. Unfortunately, I didn't have my canvas and brushes to catch the real scenes of her precious garden.

Flirtingly, I honored her royal beauty. I was in love and blossom flew within her beauty.

I couldn't figure it out why I couldn't have her for myself. Every animal complimented about her flawless beauty. Unfortunately, not even the men around her kingdom could have her. She was protected by her allies and followers.

Every animal cherished her unique walk. She had beautiful big lips and toned with her pink lip stick.

From my observation, I had the feeling she must have spent the whole day beautifying her lips (Glossy).

I admired her flawless beauty.

However, I raised my voice loudly, "Bow for this beautiful princess."

However, without her makeup, everyone still cherished her natural beauty. All the soldier ants and the animals cherished the pink lady bug in her territory.

The royal highness pink lady bug was adorned. However, not even the lions could get close to the pink lady bug's kingdom.

The pink lady bug was protected wherever she went to in the world. The pink lady was a great fighter.

She was a great combat warrior. She defeated her opponent through her invisible power. They called it a kiss of victory towards her battle. What was the kiss of victory all about? I could not figure it out myself.

She had a great shield and a sword to back up her fights against her opponents.

Honorably, I raised my voice, "Rock her world of beauty and kingdom."

However, I couldn't have that opportunity to approach her or have a conversation with her.

Unfortunately, the soldier ants and her allies stopped me to get in touch with her. I noticed the ants and every one wanted her as the bride and princess. It was more like a competition.

I heard that the pink lady bug had never gotten married to any one of her dreams. However, her father felt it would be a downfall towards her victory (sabotages).

In the kingdom, the pink lady bug had a party of celebration to reflect her victory.

Every animal and every one within the territory migrated to attend the celebration of her victory.

She was never defeated and she was very quiet in nature. Physically, she had a natural-pointed beauty.

In deed, a rare beauty of the pink lady bug was observed. Beautifully, there was a style within her signature movements. The men could not even control their eyes towards her. She had a unique walk.

Some of the men shivered, because she was very strong, fast, brave, and beautiful. She fought to reign and inherited every land in the kingdoms.

The pink lady bug had the highest title rank in her kingdom. She had a beautiful pink garment, which brought out her unique beauty.

A success of celebration was announced; I intended to attend her success of celebration.

I wasn't just a regular fighter. I was told one should be on the invited V.I.P lists. I was told that her success of celebration involved traditional games and exhibition awards.

I walked towards the front gate of the castle. Pink lady bug's castle was enormous and guarded with her soldiers.

The soldier ants were protecting and guarding her gates. These soldier ants were hefty with shield and swords at their sights. One of the guards ordered me to stay away from her territory.

The guards yelled at me,

"You must be brave to step in front of the Royal Highness Gates."

"Why are you here? Who sent you to face this Royal Highness Gates?"

I replied to the guard's questions,

"I came here to show my respect towards the Royal Highness Princess, the pink lady bug."

One of the guards ordered me to stay away from the gates of the castle.

The guards knew that I wouldn't step away.

The guards blew the trumpets. I saw the big birds aiming down from the sky. The big birds landed on the trees to protect the pink lady bug's territory. The trees shivered and the oranges fell off from the trees.

I asked myself, "Is this heaven or war 3?"

The blown horns were so loud and managed to block my ears. I realized my eyes were blinking and my veins were shivering too.

Internally, it was as if my body pulled apart in pieces. Gradually, it felt like my body was falling apart.

I whispered, "World, I'm not ready to die."

I needed to face those guards like a man.

Physically, I was shivering and sweating and one of the birds flew to me and persuaded me,

"Jump, Jump." I didn't understand! The underground hidden animals pulled my feet.

The underground animals wanted to swallow me, so I took my sword and slashed them into pieces.

The guards laughed and yelled at me; "You must be brave to have defeated these creepers."

The birds around me whispered into my ears, "bend! Bend!" I didn't understand!

Unexpectedly, the sharp mosquitoes came with their sharp tongues and pitched me at my back.

I yelled; "Ouch, My back, my buttocks." There were mosquito's bites.

"Would someone get these hungry mosquitoes out of here?"

Creatively, I needed to teach these mosquitoes a lesson.

Unexpectedly, a mosquito yelled at me, "Who's your papa?"

Did I hear a mosquito saying something towards my ears? Can a mosquito say a word like 'papa'?

Thoughtfully, it felt as if a doctor injected a needle within me. However, it ached so creatively.

Loudly, I yelled, "Nice job, mosquito, keep it up."

Fortunately, I had my sword; I slashed the heads of the mosquitoes. Those mosquito's slatted parts were still moving towards me. I wouldn't let those mosquitoes bite the heck out of me.

I just could not understand how mosquitoes without heads could be trying to bite me? I slashed the wings and the buttocks of the mosquitoes. Finally, they dropped down on the grounds.

Whew! What a relief! Except they managed and bit me so creatively. "What a great work of art from these hungry mosquitoes." Was that juicy to the mosquitoes?" "mosquitoes! stay away from me!"

Suddenly, I saw the big birds in the sky landing on the trees to protect the pink lady bug's territory.

The parrots whispered into my ears,

"Do you know every one was trying to get into the pink lady bug's kingdom?"

"You cannot attend the pink lady's celebration, Leave at once."

Angrily, I ignored the parrot's advice. I didn't want to listen to any bird's advice.

The parrots flew away. I shoved through a tunnel of the underground soil. I went through with my hard garment and sword. Successfully, I headed into the pink lady bug's territory.

Desperately, I washed and cleaned myself.

I pretended to be one of the guests at the celebration of the pink lady bug.

Pink lady bug's servant questioned me, "Your name, sir?"

I replied, "Prince Universe."

Pink lady bug's servant laughed at me.

The servant said, "You must be famous, I can't find your name, but you seem familiar."

"Check into your seat, sir."

The pink lady bug was heading to her royal seat. Every visitor and guest stood up to welcome pink lady bug. Hungrily, I ate a lot of food served and was filled up that I couldn't stand up. The crowd realized that I wasn't standing up. It was unusual for the crowd to experience this for the first time.

The crowds and audiences yelled, "He must be a stranger, Keep him in detention."

Suddenly, the pink lady servants and guards ran towards me.

"You have failed to honor our royal highness."

Pink lady bug ordered and asked,

"Release him, who sent him over here?" The crowd was silenced.

Pink lady bug asked, "Who are you and what is your name?"

I replied to Pink lady bug "Prince Universe."

She smiled, "Little Prince Universe, my charming."

She asked, "How come, I never heard of that name?"

The crowd yelled, "He is nobody, destroy him."

I yelled at the crowds, I have fought for every king and won each battle. I have worked for every king and never recognized for my title of success.

Pink lady bug laughed, "You have to fight tomorrow."

Pink lady bug laughed, "Take him to his room and feed him."

"We need to see how good he is? He claimed that he was a great fighter of the past."

The crowd yelled, "Destroy him."

The pink lady bug's servant took me to my reserved room. The guard was protecting the room which I was kept in for the night. I heard a crunchy sound within the wall.

Definitely, it was a mouse crawling beside the wall.

Mercy, mercy! It was a mouse carrying a piece of cake in its teeth.

I was thinking, "How could a skinny mouse carry a heavy piece of cake?"

I realized the cake was three times bigger than the size of the tiny mouse.

I wondered if this mouse was doing regular push-ups to gain muscle.

Unfortunately, I could not tell if this mouse had body work out routine. May be the mouse was trying to do body work outs with the cake to impress other mice (females).

Impressively, I wondered how many miles away this mouse must have stolen the piece of cake.

This mouse was sweating as if it was taking a bath. No way! A mouse was not supposed to sweat.

Surprisingly, I managed to glance at the face of the mouse.

The mouse stopped and yelled, "Mind your business lazy bone, this is my cake."

Shakily, I was surprised at the mouse's response.

"Did the mouse call me lazy bone? I must be dreaming, that could not be happening."

I thought and asked, "Can a mouse talk and was it chatting with me?"

I asked the mouse, "Who are you calling lazy bone?"

The mouse responded, "Do you think you are a great fighter?"

The mouse asked, "How many have you defeated so far lazy bone?"

The mouse yelled, "You called yourself a warrior. Take a look at your chicken legs."

The mouse mocked at me, "Those chicken legs are so fragile to fight anyone."

The mouse mocked again, "Go and add some fat into those chicken legs."

Angrily, I replied to the mouse, "Quiet, leave, go and eat your cake!"

The mouse replied, "Despite, mosquitoes have bitten you so many times, lazy bone."

The mouse mocked, "How much flesh do you have in those bones of yours?"

The mouse mocked again, "The world would see how great you are on tomorrow's battle?"

Dear readers, can you believe this mouse called me 'lazy bone'?

I meant who gave this mouse such a big mouth to call me that name. Desperately, I wanted to give this mouse serious smacking of life.

I searched everywhere and yelled, "Where is my whip?"

I dismantled the little stool which I was given to manage in the small room.

Furiously, I interrogated the mouse, "Who's your papa?"

Unfortunately, I missed and I could not get the mouse.

The problem was that the mouse was moving very fast and running everywhere. It was very hard for me to catch this mouse.

The mouse was sweating and replied, "Lazy bone, Chicken legs, beef and potato would do the job right."

I was sweating too and I asked, "How could such a tiny and skinny mouse call me chicken legs?"

"How could such a mouse have a big mouth?"

Does this tiny mouse know that I used to be a great warrior in the past?

How could a tiny mouse have so much word of Mouth (vocabulary / grammar)?

I thought and asked, "Who was feeding this mouse with so much word of mouth?"

I was referring the word of mouth as 'The grammar and vocabulary'.

I wondered how many days it took this mouse to learn all these words.

I was breathing heavily and tiredly. I couldn't catch up with this mouse.

I yelled continuously, "Would someone get me a tape or zipper to keep this mouse's mouth shut?"

At a far range, I asked the mouse about the availability of my opponent on the battle field.

The mouse ignored me and kept munching on the stolen piece of cake.

The mouse responded,

"They would probably give you a big fighter, so eat well; you need the stamina to conquer your opponent."

I wondered what the mouse was talking about. What big fighter was this mouse referring to?

It was morning. I washed my face, arms and feet. I was getting ready for my best fight to prove to the pink lady bug.

The crowd arrived and sat on their seats to watch the battle. The drummers arrived and played their drums to welcome pink lady bug. She was shaking her blossom towards the world.

The soldier ants fainted because pink lady bug was so beautiful. The servants dragged me towards the battle stage.

The Pink lady bug ordered, "Let the battles begin."

I thought, "Where is my opponent?" I couldn't see my opponent on the stage.

The audience and the crowd stared at me. I felt a loud voice in back of me.

My opponent blew me off the stage with a noise.

I looked back, "Holy mercy! It was an elephant."

No way! I give up! Despite, I was so small to face this elephant. Just a foot on me could break me into pieces. I was running for my life. How could I carry an elephant or defeat an elephant?

Oh, great! Do you know how many pounds this elephant weighs? I could have this elephant for twelve month's supper. That was a lot of food to feed on for a whole year.

I yelled loudly, "This is not my match! Stay away from me, pound smasher."

Despite, it had a lot of pounds of weight on its body. The elephant fighter squeezed my body and smashed me on the ground. My slim body felt as if it was broken and numbed.

The crowd laughed at me. I had never had such a painful spanking in my life. I had to find a way to defeat this elephant fighter.

The elephant laughed, "Why have you all brought me this to fight?"

The elephant fighter realized where I was trying to aim at his lower body section.

I headed for my sword and I used the head of my sword to hit the buttocks of the elephant fighter.

The elephant fighter blew its trunk, "Holy! My . . . ! That was an unacceptable part to hit."

The elephant screamed and fell onto the ground.

Cowardly, I thought and asked, "What was I supposed to do?"

I had to find the weakest part of this elephant and defeat this elephant fighter.

The crowd was surprised that I defeated the elephant fighter.

The pink lady bug yelled, "You have defeated one of my strongest soldiers."

"Leave and don't come back here, I have spared your life to walk away."

The crowd yelled at the pink lady bug, "let him challenge you."

The crowd yelled at me, "kiss her lips."

28

I defeated the elephant fighter and I wanted to show off my pride.

The pink lady bug was so beautiful and I wanted to kiss her on her lips.

However, there was one thing that stuck my mind. Why did they call her pink lady bug? She was a great fighter. She was a great warrior. I could see it within her gorgeous eyes.

She never used swords to defeat her opponent. She would always live forever and reign forever.

I extended my complimentary gesture towards her legacy, victory, and legendary journeys.

However, there was a myth that she was not supposed to be kissed at her lips.

I was thinking, "What did she use to defeat her opponents?"

Maybe, it had something to do with her kisses.

Unfortunately, I didn't have enough time to learn so much about her.

Definitely, I was glad that I was able to meet her and attend her party of celebration.

Gladly, I yelled, "Long lived my royal highness, the pink lady bug." I fled away from her territory.

-The end-

MY NAME IS BABAGBOSE: THEY CALLED ME

My name is Babagbose. I am very light in complexion.

Naturally, I intend to be slim and average in height (5'-8").

According to my facial description, my head was bald due to the hair-cut recommended by me from a barber shop. However, I have inherited pride from the way I appeared in nature.

Several times, I ate six times a day. Despite, I ate so much beef and potato. I still end up being slim.

One day, I was not happy the way I appeared in nature. From time to time, I appreciated my slim body.

I was never tired at anything I did in life. The ladies loved me for that reasons. However, you can all call me '**one hundred miles**' an hour (**Speed**). Kindly, check your speedometer and Excuse my language.

Dear Readers and audiences,

I need to perform some experiment towards my slim body. I need to gain some weight towards my body.

I can't believe what I was seeing in my life. Despite, I ate all the food in the fridge. Twice, I went to the store and still ended up finishing the food in the fridge.

My metabolism must be very high. Where was my food heading to? Was it my head or my arms?

I yelled, "Can I get a suggestion? A bother needs help over here."

Anyway, I need to see my doctor. My doctor could explain clearly to me.

The following morning, I called my doctor and made an appointment with him. I headed to the clinic to visit my doctor. The receptionist directed me to the waiting area. Luckily, my receptionist called my name and I walked into the doctor's office.

My appointment was approved and I headed to my doctor's office.

"Good morning, Doctor Philip."

"Good morning Mr. Babagbose, "What can I do for you today?"

I replied, "I need a medical check-up on my body weight."

My doctor checked my blood pressure and heart.

My doctor replied, "Everything seems alright with you Mr. Babagbose."

I replied to Doctor Philip, "I need to gain some weight to my skinny bones."

Doctor Philip looked at me kind of funny. He said it was natural for my body weight.

I responded to the doctor and told him that I wasn't trying to be funny by asking him those questions.

Again, I asked the doctor, "But I ate a lot of cheese, beef, chicken, and 12 foot long sub-sandwiches."

"Where was the food heading to in the past? Was it my memory?"

"Because I don't see my food consumption heading to my cheeks, hips, hands, and legs."

Dr. Philip was speechless and looked at me kind of funny.

I asked the doctor where the food consumption was heading to in my body. Doctor Philip told me to increase my food consumption everyday.

Dear readers, "Can you all believe what the doctor said to me?" I stood up and shook his hand.

I replied to the doctor, "Thanks Doctor Philip and have a nice day."

I went to the burger joint restaurant. I grabbed myself a tray and headed to the chef. I decided to order the family's menu on the lists.

I ordered 5 double cheese beef burgers, shakes, and 5 orders of fries.

The chef glanced at me and shook. The chef stared at me and I was the only one ordering a large capacity of food. The chef called his other fellow chefs to rush and prepare my dish.

The chef yelled, "We are going to make big money today, Give the big man his food."

I looked at the chef and I asked myself, "Who was he calling a big man in the restaurant?"

Despite I was a small man in the restaurant. I meant, a small man like me that can be crushed so easily with a fist. My menu order was so large and the other people in the line stared at me.

I kept hearing, "selfish, greedy dude, he eats too much, kick him out of the restaurant."

I thought to my self; nowadays, people are really hungry. I meant, take a look at the way they embarassed me just because I ordered family's meal for myself. I wanted to gain some weight to my skinny bones. I didn't care what they were saying.

The chef said kindly, "These are your orders of 5 double cheese burgers and 5 orders of fries."

I noticed that the chef said some words like '**these are your orders**'. Surprisingly, the chef knew that the food was just for me. The chef knew how to disgrace me in this restaurant.

Was the chef trying to be creative or what?

I decided to ignore every complaint received from the chefs and the people.

Glad, gracious! It was time to eat my lunch and gain some weight.

I headed to my table and ate the bunch out of myself.

"Yummy", I yelled. The sandwiches were very crunchy and delicious.

The crowd beside me at the tables stared at me.

The couples next to me asked, "Can you finish all that?"

Angrily, I ignored them, because they were getting on my last nerves.

Another guest beside me yelled at me, "You drop one gas beside me; I would break your head."

Angrily, I thought, "**Jeeezzzz**, these people were nuts."

I noticed they were asking too many questions. I wanted to enjoy my lunch and have peace of mind.

It was sad that I realized there were unfortunate people at the restaurant. I felt remorse for them. They were all glancing at my mouth as I dipped a big spoonful of ice cream into my mouth.

I thought, "Oh great, can't these people mind their businesses? They made me stain my shirt with barbeque sauce."

I thought, "How many females want a man with a barbeque sauce stained on an outfit?"

Now I looked just like a baby boy in the crib. These guests were getting on my nerves. Despite, there were some good unfortunate people at the restaurant. Some people were very quiet at the restaurant.

However, the other guests eating next to me can't seem to keep their mouths shut.

I wished I had a zipper to zip their mouths.

Angrily, I stood up and gave someone the rest of my lunch. I couldn't enjoy my lunch in the restaurant. I meant all eyes were on me and I walked out of the restaurant.

I heard one of the chefs yelled at me, "Cheap dude, no tipping for service."

However, I wished I had a sweeping broom to smack them all in the face.

I asked, "Would somebody give me a sweeping broom?" I couldn't face them all.

I meant look at the size of my body weight. How can I win this situation? I was slim and fragile. They could break me into pieces and toss me into the trash compartment (like a basket ball game).

I pointed my fist at them and ran away. Excuse my language. I was glad that I left their restaurants.

-The end-

THE SOCCER GAME

7. The Soccer Game

Audiences, Readers, Lights, cameras, and events! "Where are you all?"

I am the top player of the soccer game. Today is the day of our games. At the game stadium, we have popcorns and great ice creams.

I yelled, "Everyone is welcomed, come over. Have your seats."

There were so many crowds waiting to watch the soccer game. I was the team player and the captain.

I was ready to prove to the world that I was a great player of all times. I had the best gear to keep me energized and win this soccer game. However, we used to be the winners of the decades. Ever since I had new players on my team, we started losing the soccer game cup's season. It wasn't a series' cup game tournament. However, it was once in a year life time game season. I wanted my team to win this time in the soccer game. I wanted to win the soccer game (Golden Cup).

Being the captain of my team, I have trained my team with the best techniques. Despite, I trained my team. My team created a habit of getting weak and lazy in the soccer game.

The problem was that they wanted to score all the points. The problem was that they don't listen to me whenever I directed them to be better.

However, I gave my players an instruction on how to succeed.

Readers, I need your suggestions. The soccer game is about to begin now.

The referee blew his whistle. My goal keeper kicked the ball. One of my players in the team managed to get the ball. His name was Tony Slacker.

It was a nickname I gave him on the soccer game. The referee glanced at the players of my team.

I ask Tony Slacker to pass the ball to me. However, I was next to the great side of scoring the ball at the net. Tony ignored me and kept on playing the ball forward to score his own points. Despite, I trained my team to be the best.

Being the captain of my team, I had the rights to control the players of my team. However, I don't seem to see any improvement at all.

Accidentally, Tony Slacker bounced himself on the ball while he was playing the ball.

He hurt his feet with the ball. Was the ball controlling his body weight?

I couldn't figure it out.

The referee blew his whistle. How could this happen? I wanted the manager of my team to replace Tony Slacker. Tony Slacker was taken off from my team, because he hurt his feet and head.

I was glad my manager replaced Tony Slacker for another player within my team from the fields. The new player was Johnny and I welcomed him to my team.

The referee blew his whistle, "Let the game begin."

The goal keeper kicked the ball and Johnny managed to have the ball.

I yelled at him, "Please, Johnny, pass the ball to me over here."

Several times, I asked Johnny to pass the ball to me. Johnny ignored me and I saw him touching his stomach.

Lonely, I asked and yelled, "Why was he touching his stomach?"

Johnny dipped his hand into his pocket and started eating.

I thought to my self, "How could this happen?"

Every player on my team had different issues. I meant serious issues with different characters.

Where did they get these players from? I figured they were all rookies of the game in my team.

Would you believe me that Johnny ended up eating 3 large bags of potato chips on the fields?

However, I was expecting a miracle from my team to win the game. A miracle wouldn't appear with bags of chips. I had the feeling that heaven helps those who help themselves. I just hope he doesn't throw some gas on everybody's face.

Was he trying to be creative with the bags of chips? Mindfully, I didn't want to smell anything.

I wouldn't imagine that accident. Anything could happen on the fields. From my observation, Johnny was breathing heavily as if he wanted to swallow everyone on the field. Physically, Johnny was a big player in body weight. I hope he wouldn't blow off into pieces on the game field.

Luckily, I ran to him and asked Johnny Munch, "Give me the ball."

Johnny replied, "Don't call me '**munch**'."

Johnny started smelling like potato chips. He passes out some (creative) cologne towards my face and the rest of my players. I couldn't breath and I needed some breeze. I realized that I couldn't concentrate on the soccer ball while playing on the fields. He could have taken it to the washroom.

Johnny Munch had the biggest belly on the soccer field. I didn't want to look at his belly. He looked as if he was pregnant. He must have eaten too much of that potato chips.

I yelled, "Meah! That smelled so bad."

I yelled at the referee, "**Deodorizer! Deodorizer**! Please" The referee ran to us.

He coughed couple of times and yelled, "What is that smell, holy mercury?"

"What have you guys been eating? Take it to the washroom."

The referee blew his whistle at Johnny. Johnny's face was covered with salty potato chip crumbs.

Unfortunately, Johnny was disqualified from my team for misconduct of throwing gas into the referee's face and eating potato chips on the field."

Johnny yelled at the referee, "Give me my potato chips back."

Dear Readers, I just don't understand my team. Did I hear one of my players screaming potato chips?

What a crying baby?

Did they send me peanuts and candy eaters for my team to win this game? Was I dreaming or what?

I just couldn't understand my soccer team. They kept getting lazier all the time.

One of them sat on the soccer ball and spent the whole minutes munching on candies and peanuts.

I just don't seem to understand, what's the big deal of these candies, potatoes, and peanuts?

Confusedly, I thought,

"He sat his lazy '**a** . . . **s**' down, snacking on potato chips, and could that be a smacking breeze of relief?"

I thought, "Wow! Twenty five minutes more for the game to end."

I needed my team to score points and win the game. I wanted my team to get rid of their bad habits off the game field.

They just don't listen to me. Was something blocking their ears?

This was not easy and funny for me to handle within the game.

I was sweating and running around like a chicken on the game field. I wasn't a chicken and it wasn't funny. Definitely, I was frustrated and this wasn't like me on the fields. The other opponents against my team were doing well in the game.

The other opponents against my team scored fifteen points. My team scored nothing and still at zero point ratings.

I wished my team could pass the ball to me. I could manage to score some points for my team.

They seemed to be selfish individuals and they weren't scoring any points. They weren't helping me at all on the field.

I called on my manager of my team for a replacement to continue the soccer game.

My manager yelled at me, "I have a replacement for your team and his name is Tau Bulldozer."

I replied to my manager, "I hope he wouldn't bulldoze my face with the ball. What a name?"

My manager yelled at me, "Don't screw this game and win this trophy for me and the team."

Politely, I replied to my manager, "Yes sir."

I introduced myself to my new player (Tau Bulldozer). We shook hands and the game begun. My goal keeper kicked the ball and it flew towards the opponent against my team. Tao Bulldozer ran to the opponent that had the ball.

Tau Bulldozer whispered to the opponent against my team, "I bulldozed so many faces in the past."

'I', the captain didn't understand Tau. Tau didn't have a bulldozer with him on the fields.

I guessed that was his figure of speech. However, the opponent left the ball and ran away from Tau Bulldozer.

Luckily, Tau Bulldozer took the ball and scored so many points. Cheerfully, I was impressed that Tau Bulldozer scored so many points.

However, 'I' the captain was wondering what he whispered to one of the opponents on the fields.

I didn't care as long as he kept scoring so many points for my team. However, my team was leading the game and the opponents were angry.

My team had a score of 24 points and our opponents had a score point of 16 points.

Tao Bulldozer scored so many points that I realized he was the only one scoring the points.

Tau Bulldozer was not passing the ball to any players of my team. He didn't want to pass the ball to me and I was the captain of the team. However, we had 6 minutes for the game to be over.

My manager was very happy and he didn't care who was scoring the points as long as we are leading.

Luckily, the referee blew his whistle and my team won the game. My team was handed to soccer game cup's season. However, the players of my team were angry, because Tau Bulldozer kept the ball to himself on the fields. 'I', the captain of my team ran to Tau Bulldozer and congratulated him for making my team as the winner of the game. I shook hands with Tau Bulldozer. Tao Bulldozer shook my right hand so hard and I felt he broke one of my fingers. Unexpectedly, I felt a '**crunchy sound**' within my bones.

Angrily, I yelled, "You . . . . Art of Hero, Da_ n it, not my fingers."

Unfortunately, I wasn't going to drive home since one of my fingers was broken. I couldn't hold the soccer cup and the soccer cup was so huge. However, Tao Bulldozer held the cup with my team towards a photo shoot. Tao bulldozer managed to get all the credits due to the consequence of my injury.

Purposely, I had the feeling he broke one of my fingers to be on the front cover magazine (Media /Attention/ Endorsement).

From my observation, I wondered how many substances it consisted (gold: carat). Joyfully, we celebrated and drove off with our girlfriends and left the soccer field.

-The end-

THE KARATE COFFEE AND DONUTS

8. The karate Coffee And Donuts

Hello! Everyone, it's 6 am in the morning (Buzzing sound).

Lazily, I woke up and jumped out of my bed. I checked the wall clock. The clock was the one singing to wake me up. Definitely, it was the right time to get ready for work. I didn't feel like going to work.

Lazily, I fled to the washroom (bathroom).

I turned up the hot water and took a quick bath. I went to my bedroom and dressed up for my work.

I couldn't have time to eat my breakfast. I ran out of my house and headed to the train station. There was a coffee station at the train station. I stopped and glanced at coffee and the crispy donuts. I love donuts, but not all donuts have the same flavors and quality. In the past years, I had great donuts and great coffee.

Surprisingly, I couldn't have sample of these donuts. Unfortunately, I was not sure of this unknown donuts and coffee shop. I was so hungry and I didn't have any choice. I managed to buy a cup of coffee and some crunchy donuts.

These crunchy donuts were placed in the paper bag. Fortunately, I stepped into the express train heading to my work. I sat with one of the train passengers on the train. I was glad I could find a seat on the express train. The lady felt comfortable for me to sit beside her. I sipped couple of times from my hot cup of coffee.

I was sipping my hot coffee. The train was moving so fast and I spilled hot coffee on my clothes and body. The train was about to get to my stop signal at my work. I didn't want to get up because the coffee spilled on my dressed pants. I didn't want to get up in the presence of the passengers on the train. They probably think I wet my pants and that would be embarrassing and disgusting at my age.

I thought to myself, "I've had enough rough night not sleeping well."

"How could this happen to me on the train? Who sent this coffee and donuts to me?"

I yelled at my cup of coffee, "You dumb . . . . **a . . .s** . . . coffee? Who sent you?"

"Who sent you to embarrass me on this train?"

I yelled at my cup of coffee again, "Can I have a peace of mind on this train, Why me?"

"I would smack you in the face if you do that again?"

"Please, coffee! Donuts, don't do this to me, passengers are on the train."

Suddenly, the passengers on the train glanced at me.

The lady beside me glanced at me and asked, "Why are you talking with the cup of coffee?"

She asked me again, "Don't you know it is weird to chat with a piece of dead object."

She mocked me, "Are you speaking with your coffee and donuts?"

Unfortunately, I ignored the lady beside me. I decided to eat my donuts from the brown paper bag.

I brought out one of the crispy donuts. I took a bite from my crispy donuts. I was about to take a second bite from my donuts. The train made a hard stop at one of the train stations. My donuts flew out of my paper bag. There were crumbs of donuts everywhere on the floor. Some of the crumbs of my donuts flew into the gentlemen's suits and the ladies outfits. The passengers were mad at me because I stained their business outfits with donut crumbs and coffee spills.

One of the ladies yelled at me, "You old man? How could you spill that coffee on me?"

I replied to the lady and nodded my head,

"O lady, please don't blame me, blame the donuts for disrespecting you?"

"I warned the donuts and coffee in my hands, but they didn't listen to me."

"Judge the donuts, not me. The donuts and coffee were guilty for that incident."

The lady yelled "Did you all see how this old man spill coffee and donut crumbs on us."

The passengers yelled, "let us get him."

Readers, did she lie in my face that I spilled the coffee and donuts on the passengers? She twisted everything from '**spilling the coffee**' on her along with the passengers. I realized that she flipped the whole script on me. How did she do that thing? That could not be happening.

I yelled back at the lady and passengers, "No fighting, no fighting, my donuts and coffee were guilty."

"You can have my cup of coffee and crumby donuts in the paper bag; let us call it a day."

One of the train passengers grew stubborn on the train.

They yelled at me, "You have to dry-clean our stained business outfits or pay for the damages."

Angrily, I yelled back at the passengers, "I saw you; you stole a piece of my donuts in your mouth."

My Proof of point, "I meant it flew into your mouth while in the presence of the wind."

Again, I yelled at the passengers, "Now give me back my crumbs of donuts or let me go freely."

One of the passengers yelled at me, "Well, I accidentally swallowed it; it was in my stomach old man."

I yelled back, "then get it out, I paid for those donuts, nothing comes for free."

I yelled again, "Do you want me to tab that throat of yours to get that crumbs of donuts out?"

One of the passengers yelled, "You know that is impossible to get it out of his stomach, you savage."

The train passengers yelled at me, "Get him and Break him."

The train operator heard unbearable noises from the passengers on the train. The train operator stopped the express train at the second station. The doors of the train were opened at a wide range.

The train operator walked through the opened doors to stop the noises from the people.

The train operator asked everyone on the train, "What is wrong with you all, why on my train?"

The passengers yelled at the train operator, "This old man spilled coffee and crumbs of donuts on us."

The train operator glanced at me and asked,

"Is that true that you were responsible for all these troubles?"

For two seconds, I was speechless towards the train operator's question. I was the old man they were referring to on the train. I was speechless and I had to flip the whole script on the passengers and train operator.

I had my cold coffee and crumbs of donuts in my paper bag. I handed over my cold cup of coffee and crumbs of donuts to the train operator.

Politely, I replied to the train operator, "The coffee and donuts were guilty of this trouble."

The train operator yelled at me,

"You mean to tell me that the cup of coffee and donuts caused all these troubles on my train?"

Politely, I handed my cup of coffee and the bag of donuts to the train operator.

Politely, I begged the train operator, "Judge the cup of coffee and blame the donuts."

I ran out of the express train and headed to work so late.

I thought to myself, with all the troubles that cup of coffee and donuts did to me on that train.

Why wouldn't I run? It was embarrassing and shameful for one to experience that incident on the train.

The first incident was a coffee spill on my business pants. And the second incident was the spilling of coffee on the lady on the train.

Angrily, I asked, "Why me?" I was glad that I escaped from the passengers on the train. I noticed they could have given me serious smacking of life. I needed my face, nose, arms, legs, and feet to survive in this universe. I couldn't face them all. It was time for me to head to work and show appreciation to my old friends.

-The end-

MY RIDE: CAMEL MEJO

I had two automobiles. My first ride was an old-fashioned automobile and my second ride was camel mejo. Unfortunately, I had serious issues with the internal engine of my first ride.

Most of the time, I couldn't depend on my first ride. I was spending so much money on fuel from my first ride (automobile). I realized an automobile could be very expensive. My second ride was 'camel mejo' which I used to take to the fields on my leisure time.

Creatively, I gave my second ride a name which was camel mejo. A camel is an animal that explores around the area of a desert.

Creatively, this was the reason why I intended on giving my animal ride a nickname. It was used as a means of transportation on the fields (camel mejo).

My camel mejo car doesn't need any fuel to be driven on the road. However, it was very slow and it costs me less money to maintain on the road. I didn't have to buy fuel to make my camel mejo car move on the fields or road. I could increase the speed of my camel mejo car on the road. All I have to do is pull or pitch one of the hairs of my camel mejo car. Camel mejo would yell and move faster on the road. There was a time I rode my came mejo towards the fields. Unfortunately, I couldn't control my camel mejo on the fields. Camel mejo ran out of the fields to the express ways. From that first accident, the other car drivers on the road disliked my camel mejo car. Who cares? I obtained a car license for my camel mejo. My camel mejo was registered and I had the feeling the license insurer didn't know camel mejo.

According to my occupation, I practiced farming and agriculture on the fields. This type of occupation enabled me to maintain my camel mejo car. Five times a day, I have to feed my camel mejo car to increase energy.

Energy wise, camel mojo car needs energy to drive on the road.

I fed my camel mejo car green plants to provide energy.

The green plants supplied my camel mojo car all the nutrients, energy and the healthy resources.

As a means of transportation, I rode on my camel mejo and arrived at my final destinations.

Everyone on the road drove their real automobiles. Ever since my real automobile broke down, I depended on camel mejo. Unfortunately, I was the only one who rode the cheapest means of transportation on the road.

Dear readers, you can all call me the cheapest man on earth.

I didn't care and my broken car kept me through this scenario.

However, I responded to the car drivers, "Blame my camel mejo, my camel mejo was responsible for these accidents on the road."

Several times, I had heavy traffics on the expressway and the minor roads. The road traffic controller didn't want me to take another short route but to obey the rules and road signs.

I pitched my camel mejo's hair and it released some air gas to other drivers' noses. I realized the drivers on the road couldn't stand the smell of my camel mejo (car). The traffic aid operator couldn't stand the smell that came out of my camel mejo car. Tightly, the road traffic aid operator held her nose.

I realized that she was running from my camel mejo car.

However, the road traffic operator asked me, "I hope nothing was wrong with your camel mejo? Did you release some gas?" "Maybe that was why the camel was moving so fast on the road."

I was speechless and I was trying to twist the whole script of the accident.

I thought for a while, "How was I supposed to know that my 'camel mejo' caught a cheese (gas)?"

The road traffic aid operator asked, "I can still smell it, what was that sound again?"

The road traffic aid operator asked me again,

The road traffic aid operator yelled at me again, "That was so loud, what have you been eating?"

Respectfully, I replied, "I didn't do it; maybe camel mejo caught a cheese (gas)."

'I' the owner of camel mejo could smell it. I thought for a second, "Jeezz, It smelled so bad."

Was that smell from my camel mejo? I held my nostrils to flip the whole script on the drivers on the roads.

The road traffic aid operator yelled angrily, "This is beyond my strength, I'm out of here."

Amazingly, the cars on the expressway yielded for my camel mejo. My camel mejo car was able to pass through the traffic road. The drivers on the expressway held their nostrils which I wouldn't care.

Some of the drivers ran out from their cars. Why wouldn't they? My camel mejo car pulled up a terrific idea. My camel mejo car released some unbelievable loud gas unto their faces. It must be the green plants I was feeding my camel mejo car that pulled up the trick.

I thought for a second,

"Was it my fault? Did I know camel mejo was going to release some creative gas?"

"Don't blame me; blame the insurer that gave camel mejo the license."

Fortunately, I escaped the heavy traffic on the expressway and the road. The expressway and road were abandoned by the other car drivers. I didn't care that they didn't like my camel mejo car.

Fortunately, I was able to reach my final destination through my camel mejo. Honestly, it felt like giving myself and my camel mejo car some royal respect. I was glad my camel mejo car released some gas towards other drivers' faces on the road. The scenario was like 'make way, the Boss has arrived'. However, I intended on riding my camel mejo on the fields. My camel mejo went out of control and broke onto the road.

This was what I admired most about my camel mejo car.

I yelled at the car drivers while they ran out from their vehicles on the expressway, "who's your daddy?"

-The end-

THE DR. PEPPER RESTAURANT

The Animal kingdom

10. The Dr. Pepper Restaurant

Romantically, it was morning and I saw beautiful couples hugging each other. I was there at my restaurant. I was having a cup of coffee and reading the daily news papers.

Lonely, I thought, "How romantic? I needed a hug and that made me feel like crying.

Sadly, I thought, "Where are the single ladies?"

I glanced through the windows of my new restaurant. From my observation, some people were passing by and heading to work. I opened a new restaurant at the corner of the street. It was a restaurant that served soup of the day. I was the owner of the second new restaurant in town. My first restaurant was doing well at other foreign location.

I decided to open and launch a second restaurant in town. My soups of the day at my restaurant served healthy rich ingredients; it consisted of red pepper, diced carrots, and mushrooms and grilled chicken strips. Definitely, one should taste and experience the soups of my restaurant.

Respectfully, I brought out my flyers and gave them to the people walking by my new second restaurant.

It was my way of creating awareness of my new second restaurant. I called it advertising and it was working for me.

I was the owner and I announced my grand opening to the public,

"Hello readers and audience, welcome to my new restaurant."

"The name of my new restaurant is Dr. hot pepper restaurant."

'I' the owner, thought to myself, "Would you blame me for opening my new restaurant? Despite, everyone needs to eat food at the restaurant."

"Can you all believe me that I still own a second new restaurant in town?"

Dr. hot pepper restaurant serves healthy soups for customers who love soups. I placed a sign board in front of my new restaurant. I felt that was the only way to let the community know that I was hiring a chef for my new restaurant. I wanted to travel to the overseas and experience other great dishes of the world.

Desperately, I needed to travel out of the country to the overseas. I heard there was a good chef in town. Fortunately, I hired a chef to take over my new second restaurant.

His name was Chef Joe.

The new chef arrived at my second new restaurant. I explained to him how I wanted my new restaurant to be operated.

I explained to him that hospitality comes first with the customers.

Hospitality is the first priority when dealing with customers. However, Smiling and great facial expressions were the keys to succeed in the business world. And that was how I expanded my restaurant business. Successfully, my restaurant business had been doing well. During my first opening, I gave out free sample of my recipe hot soups to the customers. It was a way for me to create awareness of my new restaurant to the public.

My soup menu was designed to make my customers energized. Some customers complained about their sore throats. My hot spicy soup made their sore throats relieved and that was one of the advantages of my soup recipes. My customers were allowed to take five sips of my soup recipes. My hot spicy soup solved everyone's problems.

I was the owner of Dr. Pepper restaurant. And I was glad to invite great customers to my new restaurant. I welcomed my new chef to my new restaurant. The next day, I traveled out of the country.

The new chef was in charge of my new restaurant while I was out of the country. And I couldn't monitor my new chef while I was gone. I felt my new chef would do a great job at my new restaurant.

My new chef brought one of his old giant bells to my new restaurant. Twice, he rang the bell and yelled loudly in front of my restaurant.

The new chef yelled, "The soups are ready and free, come and celebrate with me at this restaurant."

The customers rushed in to my new restaurant and they were served to their delights.

'I', the owner of the restaurant was not there to experience everything.

At my restaurant, the new chef told one of his friends that he claimed he was a great chef.

Definitely, I was not there to hear what he was saying. However, he dressed up like a great chef when I interviewed him and hired him.

How could I tell? I was so busy travelling around the world to learn food recipes. During my absence, my new chef mistakenly told people that he hardly knew about food and restaurant.

My new chef yelled, "I told my boss that I was a great cook, and my boss believed me."

"I told my boss that I prepared delicious soups for customers and my boss believed me."

At my second new restaurant, one of the customers complained the soup was too spicy. However some customers managed to drink water to calm off the hotness of my new chef's dishes. Several times, the customers had problems running to the washroom. Several times, the customers sneezed because my new chef's soup dishes were not prepared well. I wondered how many gallons of hot sauce he used for the soups. I hope my new chef wasn't sending my customers to the clinic. A great friend of mine was informing me through the phone on how my restaurant was doing in town.

Definitely, my new chef could have added surplus of grinded red pepper to the soup recipe. Excessive pepper in soups was a sign of going to the washroom all the time. In my absence, my new chef made another announcement to the public.

My new chef announced to the public, "Come and taste the special soup of the day?"

My new chef yelled again, "Dine in and come on in, the kitchen is open."

One of the old customers yelled at my new chef, "Are you nuts?"

My new chef ignored my old customers at my restaurant. Desperately, my new chef taught my customers on how to prepare soup recipes. My new chef broke the rules of my new restaurant and turned my restaurant up-side down.

Awfully, can you all believe this new chef decorated my second new restaurant while I was gone?

My new chef invited new customers to my restaurant kitchen. My new chef gave the customers my cooking hardware. He lit up the stove for the customers to take control of my kitchen.

My new chef gave the customers the menu list and watched them prepare their soups in my kitchen.

My new chef created a small musical section for entertainment. There was a small zoo amusement section at the restaurant which I would never recommended anyone. There were animals playing drums as a source of music for my customers. My new chef brought uninvited guests and unwelcomed animals to my new restaurant.

My new chef created a source of entertainment for my customers and I was not there.

'I' the owner was thinking, "Who was giving this new chef these ideas?"

However, I was getting sources of information on the phone about my new restaurant.

Some customers complained that the songs were too tradition.

From other sources, I overheard that one of the animals broke into the stage and danced to the music.

What types of animals were at the restaurant or stage? Was this an animal kingdom, zoo, or what?

I had the feeling my restaurant must be disorganized. Maybe it was time for me to leave the overseas and investigate my new restaurant.

"I, the owner, thought, "I was not there to experience everything at my new restaurant."

I was out of my place of living and learning other great soup recipes. I was too busy not paying attention to my new restaurant which I left for the new chef. I received a phone call from one of my friends in town.

I was informed that my restaurant was filled up with animals. I couldn't understand my friend's explanation on the long distant phone. I thought they said that my new chef bought a high definition screen to entertain my guests.

However, I gave my new chef some back-up funds to use for my new restaurant (emergency purpose).

I wanted to know if my friends were telling me the truth about my new restaurant.

I felt embarrassed about what they told me on the phone. I made a long distant phone call and my new chef picked it up on that same day. My new chef was terrified that I called to find out how my new restaurant was doing. I could hear sounds of animals and series of music and drum sounds. I had strange feelings that there were kangaroos, singing birds, honey bees, and others.

I asked myself, "Was that a zoo or my second new restaurant that I overheard?"

Already it was night, I was thinking of booking my next flight. The following morning,

I booked my flight to see how my second new restaurant was doing. Desperately, I had to leave the foreign country. I didn't want to jeopardize my restaurant business. Safely, I managed to arrive in town.

Some of the animals were performing shock-dancing and some were drinking beers. One of the kangaroos was learning how to kick-box each other. I saw a grasshopper munching on maize in the kitchen of my new restaurant. I saw the bees manufacturing honey from the hives in my kitchen.

Angrily, I yelled loudly, "Chef Joe! Where are you?" "This couldn't be my new restaurant."

This couldn't be my new restaurant serving beers and weird animals taking over my restaurants.

I yelled loudly and asked, "Where are the humans . . . .?"

Chef Joe was not around in my restaurant. Fortunately, someone in the neighborhood told me he went to order more drinks for the animals. I wondered if he was spending my flexible account of my new restaurant.

I yelled at the animals and ordered them to leave my new restaurant. The kangaroos opened their mouths and flashed their white teeth at me.

Angrily, I snapped at the animals, "I don't want to see your white teeth, Get out of my restaurant."

Several times I yelled, "animal kingdom stay away from me, please stay away from human beings.

Angrily, I yelled at the kangaroos and threw a bucket at them. The kangaroos escaped the bucket and jumped on the bucket. The flying bees wrote a sign with honey and ordered me to leave the restaurant.

Angrily, I snapped at the bees, "Not in my face, I still own this restaurant."

I yelled, "Who taught these bees how to write?"

Suddenly, I smacked the kangaroo's head with a large hot cooking utensil.

I managed to smack another two to three chickens on their heads. These healthy chickens had natural crowns and I observed it through the heads.

Sparingly, the kangaroo held its head tightly and yelled back at me,

"Yaaa, yayah, My head."

I, the owner waited and thought for a second, "**Yaaa, yayah,** My head."

I was thinking, "What does 'yaaa! yaya' mean? What a language?"

"Was that in the dictionary or was that a new vocabulary?"

Surprisingly to myself, I wondered how these animals interact.

I was thinking maybe the hot spoon was not boiling enough in the animal's brains.

Angrily, I yelled at the animals, "I will give you more life burning on your nose with this hot spoon."

The animals ran out and escaped. I was sure the animals won't come back to the kitchen of my restaurant. I gave them serious hot smacking of life. These animals would learn how to respect the human beings at presence of time.

The entire kitchen was disorganized with broken chairs, tables, and cooking utensils.

Who gave these animals permission to take over my restaurant?

Chef Joe arrived at my restaurant. He found that I was at the restaurant. Chef Joe realized that I was chasing the animals out while he was gone to grocery store. He found that the animals were gone and out of my restaurant. Chef Joe noticed there wasn't availability of music in my restaurant. Painfully, I stepped out of the kitchen with a bandage on my left arm.

Surprisingly, Chef Joe gnashed his teeth and stared at me.

Chef Joe stammered, "Are you alright Boss?"

I replied to Chef Joe's question, "Well the animals made a **'boss'** out of my face and arm."

It was not funny and I was really mad at how Chef Joe corresponded to my questions.

Angrily, I glanced at Chef Joe,

You crazy chef, "See what you have done to my pricey restaurant. Where are all my customers?"

"Who sent you to operate my new restaurant with these animals?"

Chef Joe replied, "Boss, I didn't bring in any animal to your restaurant"

Chef Joe asked, "Boss, did you send these animals out of your restaurant?"

I gnashed my teeth at Chef Joe,

"You were the one that invited these animals to my restaurant while I was out of the country."

I yelled madly, "You crazy chef, you have to pay for all these damages."

Chef Joe replied, "The animals are coming back in 3 seconds."

I yelled back, "What do you mean the animals are coming back?"

Chef Joe replied, "Sir, can't you hear your restaurant vibrating?"

I yelled at Chef Joe, "Why is my restaurant vibrating now?"

One of the animals yelled, "It's payback time."

The parrots were screaming, "It's payback time."

I was surprised to see the animals coming back to my new restaurant.

I realized there were big cows with heavy ropes attached to the building of my restaurant.

I was angry at the whole situation. Maybe the hot cooking spoons weren't doing the job for me.

I wanted the animals to be gone forever.

Despite, I gave the kangaroos a creative smacking on the head.

I also smacked the stubborn chickens and birds out of my restaurant. I noticed the feathers of the chickens were flying everywhere in my restaurant.

I didn't expect them to come back to my restaurant. I wanted the animals to learn and respect the human beings.

Gradually, my new restaurant started falling apart and it was breaking into pieces. I wondered what was moving the building of my new restaurant off the ground.

Chef Joe replied, "We need to run out of here unless the building would collapse on us."

Chef Joe and I ran out of my new restaurant.

The kangaroo gave orders to other animals. The honey bees were heading towards me. I didn't want the bees to sting me.

"1, 2, 3, 4 . . . go!" One of the kangaroos turned backs at me and yelled,

"It's pay back time, **Take this**!"

One of the kangaroos threw some heavy punches toward my face.

Surprisingly, I realized one of my teeth flew out of my mouth.

Angrily, I asked, "Was this a therapy or disaster?

I thought for a while, "Was that why the kangaroos were training from kick-boxing?"

Angrily, I thought, "Did my new chef bring these kangaroos to take over my new restaurant?"

However, Chef Joe claimed he didn't invite the animals to my restaurant. He deserved to be a great lawyer and I couldn't prove him wrong. I couldn't hold him responsible for all the damages.

I yelled at Chef Joe, "Get me a medication for my teeth." Chef Joe ignored me and scratched his head.

I held my mouth and I managed to yell at the animals. However, the animals broke in and pulled down my restaurant.

Surprisingly, Chef Joe was not helping me at all and he was just standing there. Creatively, Chef Joe shook there like a jelly fish. I couldn't wait to get my hands on him for his mischief.

'I' the owner of my new restaurant was speechless for 10 seconds.

Again, I yelled at the animals, "Stop! No! Not my restaurant."

My restaurant was demolished by the big cows with the heavy ropes.

The kangaroos laughed at me and ran away! This wasn't funny and the animals were laughing at me.

I glanced at my restaurant and it was all gone. These animals demolished my pricey new restaurant.

Chef Joe looked at me and yelled at me,

"Boss, I saved your life, your new restaurant has been demolished."

"Boss, you should compliment me for saving your life and getting you out of there."

Chef Joe yelled again, "Those animals were wild and creative, What a creative work?"

Chef Joe asked again, "How could they do something like that, your new restaurant is gone?"

Creatively, Chef Joe asked again, "Where did they get that kind of strength from?"

For fifteen seconds, I was speechless towards Chef Joe's words of irritation. I was the owner and He twisted the whole script on me. How did he do that? I couldn't compete with Chef Joe. Someday in the future, He deserved to be a great lawyer.

Dear Readers,

Can you all believe my new restaurant was destroyed by Chef Joe and the crazy animals?

Instead, Chef Joe kept on chatting with me with his pathetic words of irritation. He was pretending as if he wasn't responsible for the downfall of my new restaurant. He invited those animals into my new restaurant, while I was gone to the overseas to learn different dishes of the world.

Chef Joe questioned me, "Boss, see what you have done to your new restaurant, it's gone."

Angrily, I yelled at Chef Joe, "You are responsible for the downfall of my new restaurant."

Chef Joe asked, "Why did you hire those animals to take over your restaurant?"

Angrily, I yelled back at Chef Joe, "You hired those crazy animals while I was gone."

"You brought those crazy animals to my new restaurant while I was gone to the overseas."

Several times, I missed smacking Chef Joe's head with one of the cooking utensil at my hand.

Chef Joe projected towards the cooking utensil which was held at my hand.

Chef Joe yelled at me, "No! Not on my head!"

Several times, I managed to smack his head with the cooking utensil which was held at my hand. Chef Joe's head was five feet swollen in height. From my observation, It was swollen enough to build a bridge or a tower. However, the construction workers were welcomed to use his swollen head to build the bridges.

Unfortunately, Chef Joe managed to escape. I yelled at Chef Joe while he was running away.

"You crazy chef, you ruined my new restaurant, come here and fix this place up."

-The end-

MY WEALTHY DONKEYS: THE DIARY

11.) My Wealthy Donkeys

My name is Babagobose and I own two donkeys in my yard at my hut house. These donkeys earned me funds to maintain my farming (occupation). I was able to pay my taxes on what I earned from my donkeys.

Several times, I took my donkeys for rides at the beach. At the beach, Customers rode on my donkeys.

My donkeys made me wealthy because I had so many customers. I negotiated with my donkeys by feeding more healthy green plants. I became very wealthy and greedy to my donkeys.

However, one of my donkeys communicated with me but I couldn't understand. I was human and these were animals that lived within my yard. I just couldn't understand the languages these donkeys were speaking. Literately, I wished my donkeys could write it down for me to understand.

I noticed that my donkeys were glancing at me with widely opened teeth.

Several times, I asked myself, what were they trying to tell me?

From my observation, my donkeys were very scary looking. I hope these donkeys would not bite my face off. Cowardly, I moved my back and buttocks a few step away from my donkeys.

I wouldn't allow any donkey bite off my nose from my face. I need my face for life to survive.

Surprisingly, take a look at the way these donkeys were eating the green plants. I realized my donkeys were biting so hard on the green plants.

I thought, "**Jeeeeez**! Do donkeys eat like this? Just don't bite my face."

My donkeys weren't eating enough. My donkeys were not eating the green plants which I was feeding them.

Someday, I felt my donkeys were going to bite me. In the past, my donkeys used to be big and healthy.

Recently, my donkeys seemed to be getting skinnier and smaller in body weight. There was a time I took my donkeys to the beach to earn for more funds. One of the customers was so big in size and my donkeys ran away. The same customers complained to me that my donkeys were too skinny to carry them.

I raised a question, "How could this happen to me?"

Despite, I fed my donkeys with more green plants to gain some weight.

These donkeys were my only means for surviving in this world. I also cultivated this great idea as a source of extra income. I survived through the presence of my donkeys. However, these donkeys have given quality uncountable rides to the customers at the beach.

I didn't want my business to stop operating and I needed to survive. I decided to do some shopping lists for my donkeys.

I stepped out of my house and headed to the shopping mall.

I bought some head garments for my wealthy donkeys (the crowns).

I referred the 'gold crowns' as a head gear.

I placed them on my donkeys to attract more customers.

My donkeys threw them away and stepped on the crowns. Surprisingly, my donkeys were so mean to me.

I have never experienced this before in my life. I asked myself, "What do these donkeys want?"

I flashed one of my funds and placed it within the mouths of my donkeys. My donkeys were jumping around and hitting the walls of my yard.

I raised a question for a second, "Were these donkeys trying to get paid too?"

This couldn't be happening to me? These donkeys were just animals and not humans. How could these donkeys be interested in my earnings and funds? Who taught these donkeys about currency?

Who lectured these donkeys? I realized there were golden crowns while I was counting my funds. I was thinking how my donkeys obtained these golden crowns.

The golden crowns of my donkeys were shining so hard and it almost made me blind.

I screamed so loudly, "Ahhhhhhhhhhh!"

My donkeys ignored me and didn't want me to touch the Golden crowns. I left my donkeys alone and rested at home for the whole day.

The next morning of the day, I tried to compromise with my donkeys.

Unfortunately, my donkeys couldn't speak because they were animals. Desperately, I was willing to negotiate with my donkeys. I succeeded in negotiating with my donkeys to work for me. My donkeys were willing to offer rides for my customers. I fed my donkeys with healthy plants and some water to digest the food consumption. Successfully, I was able to have bread and fried egg for breakfast. I drank a cup of tea and I was filled up to my satisfaction.

Career wise, I was able to cultivate some maize at my farming land. I removed some unwanted plants from the enriched soil. I spread water on my crops. This made the crops to grow at a faster time. It was getting to evening for the whole day. I went home to get the donkeys ready for work. I dragged my two donkeys to the beach.

I was waiting for customers to ride on my donkeys. Fortunately, a customer was willing to ride on my donkeys. Several times, I took photographs while they sat on my donkeys.

However, my donkeys were misbehaving when I was about to take a requested pictures from the customers. I realized my donkeys were not smiling at me and my customers. I realized my donkeys were showing off these golden crowns in the pictures. Carelessly, I wasn't paying attention to these golden crowns. I was focusing on the customers in the pictures. Tiredly, I skipped the entire situation.

According to the snaps of the pictures of my customers, I felt embarrassed and tried to control my donkeys.

However, my donkeys were very stubborn. Unfortunately, I found it hard to control my donkeys.

The customers had few rides from my donkeys at the beach. Some couples had their pictures taken with rides from my donkeys.

I made extra funds and paid some taxes from my wealthy donkeys' investment.

At the end of the day, I dragged my donkeys to my house. I tipped my donkeys some funds, because they earned me funds for the evening. I was getting tired of my wealthy donkeys.

My wealthy donkeys were raising the price of my tips I gave them.

I gave my donkeys a tip from my funds. However, my donkeys rejected what I gave out as an extra tip.

Several times, I gave my donkeys three tips and it was accepted. I realized these donkeys were getting more intelligent than ever.

I raised a question, "Was someone behind these donkeys?"

"Who was feeding information to my donkeys?"

There was one thing I realized about my donkeys. I realized my wealthy donkeys were very happy whenever I watch television.

There was a time I was watching television, my wealthy donkey pushed their heads through the window.

I realized that they obtained their knowledge from the television. All the videos I watched must have educated my wealthy donkeys. As a source of information, this was where my donkeys obtained the golden crowns.

I wondered who had given my donkeys those golden crowns.

I yelled loudly, "Illusion, I was supposed to be the one with a golden crown."

I found cans of gold spray paints and some writings on pieces of papers indicating; "Have these funds and give me more golden items."

I wondered who had written those words for my wealthy donkeys.

I decided to hide my windows from my wealthy donkeys.

My donkeys nodded heads and begged me not to take the television shows away.

I decided to take a walk at the beach with one of my wealthy donkeys. My donkey gave me a kick at my feet.

I shivered and asked, "A kick, what was that all about?"

I was wondering why my donkey did that to me.

Again, my donkey kicked me twice to look around me.

I screamed, "Ouch! My leg hurts."

Then a beautiful lady walked towards my aid.

She was so beautiful looking and I realized that could be the reasons why my donkeys kicked me.

Shyly, she asked for my name and I replied, "My name is Kofi, and yours?"

She replied, "Angela is my name."

My wealthy donkeys smiled and I compromised with my wealthy donkeys (occupation).

I bought a new television for my donkeys so that they could watch more videos.

Definitely, my wealthy donkeys were happy and I earned more funds with the help of my donkey's rides at the beach.

My new girlfriend Angela stayed with me and we held hands at the beautiful sight of the beach.

-The End-

GETTING OLD

12.) Getting Old

Peacefully, it was morning and I was awakened. I was still feeling sleepy. Why was I feeling so sleepy and tired?

Was it because I was getting old? Maybe I needed to add daily exercise to my routine.

Maybe I was not taking my daily multi-vitamins at the right dosage. I was just feeling tired in my body.

Unfortunately, my feet, toes, fingers, and back felt so weak. However, I used to be very energetic and strong when I was in my 20's. Despite my body hurts so badly, I just hope my body won't fall apart.

Physically, I needed my body parts to function in life.

Despite of my bad habit, I used to bite the nails of my fingers.

However, I left all my bad habits behind and cultivated new ideas in life. I cultivated an idea of drinking ten cans of sodas every day. However, I was not able to finish the cans of sodas. The flies managed to consume the left over in the can. Despite of my new habit, I usually open 10 cans of sodas in a roll on the table. Gradually, I drank each can of sodas in my sitting room.

Several times, I drank while I watched sports on my television. It was a 'drink and sleep' daily routine.

I was not happy with the new cultivation of my ideas. I needed something to keep me busy. I needed some fresh air and I drove to the coffee shop. I stepped out of my car and walked towards the front door of the coffee shop.

Suddenly, a customer ran out of the coffee shop.

She yelled at me, "Don't order, and don't use the washroom, leave!"

I looked at her eyes and ignored her warnings. Despite, my stomach was speaking "hunger."

There were three customers in the line to order their breakfasts. Desperately, I joined the queue after three customers. I arrived to be customer no. 4 in the queue. I was feeling so hungry and I was looking for a great idea to get my food ordered.

The three customers were taking their time at the ordering section. However, I couldn't hold my hunger any longer. I whispered into the ears of one of the customers before me within the queue.

I whispered at customer no. 3, "Dear sir, there's a big mountain of dog's bubbles at the back of your shirt."

Then customer no.3 yelled, "I have to leave the coffee shop and thanks for telling me."

Then customer no.3 handed his ordering ticket into my hand and ran out of the coffee shop.

He must have felt embarrassed by what I told him. Who cares? I was getting closer to my order.

I didn't need his ticket. I wasn't going to eat what he ordered on the menu. Not my kind of breakfast.

I still have three customers in the queue at the ordering section. I needed to come up with another idea.

I walked closer to customer no.2 and whispered into his ears.

I whispered, "Sir, there's a big nasty fly on your head, taking its time and releasing some bubbles."

Then customer no.2 whispered back, "Thank you, do you have a mirror on you?"

I replied to customer no.2, "You might want to go to the washroom and check the mirror."

Then customer no. 2 whispered,

"No! I don't want anybody making fun of my head and I have to go now."

Then customer number 2 handed his ordering ticket into my hand and ran out of the coffee shop.

The owner of the coffee shop noticed the customers were running out of his coffee shop. He walked closer to me and interrogated me.

The Owner asked, "Who sent you? Why are you here? Why are my customers leaving my coffee shop?"

I replied to the owner, "They had serious stomach issues and they had to leave."

The owner of the shop yelled, "I am watching you and don't cause any mischief."

The owner of the shop walked away and sat on his chair.

Readers and audience, what was I supposed to do? I was hungry and the food service was so slow.

The owner of the shop believed that I chased the customers out of his coffee shop.

However, customer number 1 was still in the queue taking his time and ordering his breakfast.

I yelled, "People, people, what is taking so long to order a breakfast?"

"Do you all worship breakfast in this coffee shop? I have been in the queue for almost 50 minutes."

Several times, the owner of the coffee shop walked closer to me and yelled at me.

"I knew you were a trouble maker immediately you stepped into my coffee shop."

The shop owner yelled at me, "What's your problem?"

The owner yelled, "The service chef has not finished preparing the breakfast for customer no. 1."

Being one of the customers within the queue, I managed to ignore the shop owner. However, I was speechless for minutes. I was scratching my head and the food service was taking so long.

Unfortunately, I was so tired of standing for long in the queue. I sat down on one of the chairs in the coffee shop. However, I was told the owner of the shop had a dog in the washroom of his coffee shop.

I wondered why he would hide his dog in the washroom.

Definitely, he must be nuts. Why would I go to the washroom with an unknown dog?

I rather use the washroom alone than sharing it with an unknown dog. Definitely, I needed my privacy in the washroom.

I couldn't believe customer no. 1 was still waiting for his breakfast. May be I should go to another coffee shop for breakfast. The food chefs were moving as if they had unavailability of bones in their bodies.

There was one thing I noticed about this coffee shop. It was obvious that the two food chefs were inexperienced. They were nervous and sweating in the kitchen. They had badges on their uniforms indicating few words; novice, please endure.

I thought, "How long do I have to endure to have my breakfast ready, 3 hours?"

I ordered a cup of coffee with egg, cheese, and bacon on a toasted wheat bagel. I felt like taking over the kitchen.

My head was boiling and my eyes were brewing red coffee. Excuse my language.

I was the customer and I yelled at the coffee store,

"Who's the boss? Who's your papa? Give me the kitchen, let me take over!"

My stomach was getting real hot and I ran towards the washroom of the coffee shop.

As I was running towards the door of the washroom, I noticed the washroom was vibrating.

Unpredictably, I thought it was an earthquake or tornado.

I stepped into the washroom and I saw a mighty dog roaming around the washroom.

There was a sign tied on the neck of the mighty dog.

The sign was indicating; 'don't wet the floor, please, keep it clean'.

I asked, "What? Did they keep a dog in the washroom to be watching my bu . . . t . . . . k?"

Several times, the mighty dog barked at me and I yelled back, "Dog, leave, I need my privacy."

As I was using the mini washroom, I noticed the mighty dog was making sure I don't wet the floor.

I raised a question, "Who sent this mighty dog to me?"

Despite, this mighty dog was nuts and annoying. I felt like kicking the dog's face out of the washroom.

However, I was so small to face this enormous dog.

"**Jeeez** . . . ! Where did they get such a **muscular species** from? This dog looked so enormous."

"Was this dog working out at the health club?"

"Maybe I should just step out of this washroom."

Honestly, this was the ugliest dog that I have ever seen in my life. Excuse my language.

Accidentally, the floor of the washroom was damped at several times. The mighty dog bit my khaki pants and barked.

I screamed, "Ouch, my bu . . . t . . . . k, my khaki pants, what the . . . .?"

I couldn't believe that mighty dog in the washroom torn my khaki pants.

I couldn't believe that mighty dog flipped me through the walls.

I yelled at the dog, "Did I know I was going to wet the floor of the washroom?"

Horribly, I couldn't use the toilets any more. I pulled up my khaki pants and ran out of the washroom.

The customers were laughing at me.

I screamed at them, "This is not funny, look at my torn pants."

I ordered one of the customers, "Get me a doctor."

Angrily, I yelled at them, "there is an ugly dog in there; it bit my bu . . . to . . . ks."

Again, I yelled at the customers, "you are all nuts."

Disappointedly, I decided to step out of the coffee shop to see a doctor. I saw a new customer who walked into the coffee shop. And I tried to tell the customer what happened.

I tried to warn the new customer but he wouldn't listen to me.

I yelled at the new customer, "Sir, leave this shop." Ignorantly, he ordered his menu.

He probably didn't know the coffee shop had serious issues with their services.

Suddenly, the coffee shop owner arrived at his shop and he walked towards me.

The coffee shop owner yelled at me, "What did you do to my washroom?"

I replied to the shop owner, "Take a look at what your dog did to me, torn clothes?"

The coffee shop owner yelled and asked, "What dog? Did you bring any dog to the washroom?"

I responded to the coffee shop owner,

"You are all nuts, that dog had a sign tag indicating; 'don't wet the floor, please, keep it clean'.

Angrily, I asked the coffee shop owner, "Weren't you the one that put that warning sign in your washroom?"

The coffee shop owner was speechless and clueless. I had the feeling he was trying to hide his guilty conscience. He knew that dog belongs to him. He didn't want to admit that he was wrong.

I guess this was a '**case dismissed**' scenario and I had to leave the shop. I felt like a fool at the coffee shop.

Again, I yelled at the coffee shop owner and chefs "You all, going to pay for this, I'm getting a doctor?"

Angrily, I left the coffee shop and drove off.

-The end-

THE GOLD TROPHY TRAIN

I love the gold trophy train. The gold trophy train was very entertaining. The gold train made me laughed whenever I was miserable and depressed. Every morning, I had the opportunity to hear people nagging on their cell phones. However, some people were making up on their cell phones.

It was like listening to 'the morning news' when heading to my destination.

Pleasantly, there was a sign of love on the gold trophy train.

However, it was morning; I headed to the train to perform my job routine. I paid my fare and sat on the seats on the gold trophy train. There was a lady beside me who was taking her time. I noticed she was putting on a lip stick on her lips and makeup on her face.

She was smacking her lips and having a fashion show on the gold trophy train. It was like a fashion show.

I didn't blame her; she wanted to look good in her appearance.

I thought within me, smack that lips, baby. I wished I could sponsor a fashion show for her in town.

She was so cute with those big lips. This was what I admired most about these ladies.

They intended to show off their beauties wherever they go in the world. They were everywhere and you could not ignore their flawless beauties. I wasn't the only one on the gold trophy train.

Despite, I can only have one wife at a time. That was my own belief in life.

I realized that there were so many people on the gold trophy train. They intended on taking the gold trophy train to work and schools. I didn't care about those ones having daily dramas on their cell phones.

I described those dramatic days like a '**girlfriend punching her boyfriend on the face**' with boxing gloves. I had the feeling it was an act of cheating dilemma against each other. However, he wasn't going to win the battle.

He should allow his girlfriend to win the battle (argumentation).

Desperately, I had my earphones and listened to some songs. I wanted to mind my business and head to work.

There was a passenger on the train in front of me. I realized this passenger was smacking his sandwich as if he was molding a clay. Was that a work of art or pottery?

I realized the passenger was biting his sandwiches so hard as if he wanted to swallow the world. I observed he had five sandwiches in a big sack. Every fifteen minutes, he swallowed each sandwich in his mouth. However, he wasn't chewing his sandwiches.

He took some huge bites from his sandwiches. I couldn't have done what he did on that gold trophy train and I wasn't that perfect.

No offence, he was enjoying his breakfast. I realized his stomach was getting bigger and bigger.

I wanted to stand up and find another seat on the train. Unfortunately, all the seats were taken by other passengers on the train.

I knew something was going to happen on the gold trophy train. Definitely, I needed a deodorizer on the gold trophy train. I didn't want to smell anything on the train. I had the feeling the passenger was going to do it on the gold trophy train.

I was referring to the amount of sandwiches that he consumed on the gold trophy train.

However, I didn't care about those 'smacking issues' on his sandwiches. It was so loud and everyone could hear it on the gold train. Despite I had my earphones; I could still hear those crunchy sounds and it was annoying. Again, he wasn't chewing on his sandwiches and it was hard to believe.

I managed to put on my dark shades because it felt as if he wanted to bite my face off. I guessed the sandwiches must be juicy. I wondered where the sandwiches were purchased. It was twice bigger than I thought. I hope he wouldn't throw it at my face. Definitely, my face would get swollen if thrown towards my face.

Despite, I was the cheapest man on earth. Unfortunately, I didn't have health insurance to bill any injury. Holy mercury, these sandwiches were as heavier than I thought.

I could tell by the way he was holding his sandwich so tightly.

Readers, "Was he biting, gulping, swallowing or what?"

I just couldn't tell which one. I couldn't get a clue.

On the left section of my seat of the train, a girlfriend was yelling at her boyfriend.

Ten minutes later, they made up and smiled at each other. How great they made up and cuddled up together.

They weren't throwing punches at each other on the gold trophy train.

This was what I love about life. I thought, it was amazing how situations could reflect in seconds and at different angles.

I thought, "Gradually, We learn in the process of life."

"Gradually, we fall at first and get stronger in the process of life."

Joyfully, I arrived at my train station stop. I needed to get out of the gold trophy train. I stepped out of the gold trophy train and landed on the platform.

Few seconds later, I heard the passengers complaining, screaming, and yelling at each other on the gold trophy train. I had the feeling it was the passenger that was gulping his sandwiches.

I was glad I left the gold train before he polluted the air on the gold trophy train (gas). I realized he did it on everyone's clothes on the gold train.

Defensively, thanks to the gold trophy train for making my day. I arrived at work on time and began my daily work routine.

-The End-

THE DATE

It was early in the morning; I woke up and rushed to the washroom. I needed to rush to the washroom. I had the feeling I had too much drinking and food last night.

Whew! It felt so good to use the washroom. The veins in my head had chilled down.

I thought, "What a relief." Now, I needed to spray some air freshener in the air.

I whispered, "Dear Readers, can I get an air freshener or breeze over here?"

I asked, "**Jeeez**, What did those chefs put in the food that made my washroom smell so bad?"

"Jeezz, indeed, it was so bad." My stomach needs some medical checkup. I wondered if it was normal for one to smell this bad after using the washroom. Truthfully, it must be normal. Gratefully, I extended my complimentary gesture towards the scientists that created the air freshener. However, I felt they should create an air freshener for the stomach too.

I glanced at the wall clock and I had 2 hours to get ready for work.

I picked up my toothbrush and paste. I brushed my teeth and took a quick shower.

I wiped myself with the towel. I performed thirty push-ups on the floor. However, my arms were getting bigger and bigger.

"Yes, indeed, Ladies admired those appearances on me."

I yelled at myself, "Work on those arms very hard, **100** miles an hour, **Speedo**".

"That was me; I was referring to myself, Pardon, my language."

Loneliness and boredoms were present in my life. Sadly, I didn't have anybody to chat with in my life.

The fact was that I was trying to stay away from trouble of life. I was referring to the dramatic days of life. Accidents whereby a companion gets caught cheating with a girlfriend. The fact was that I always headed that way whenever I date these beautiful ladies. What do you expect? These were beautiful ladies. I was referring to high quality ladies that were hard to find in life (good characters).

One of their ex-boyfriends tried to knock me down.

How was I supposed to know that she had a boyfriend or ex-boyfriend?

The good news was that I fled away from every situation before it gets out of control.

I was a small guy and I couldn't fight any battle. However, I escaped every fist of life (Speedo). Enough of my words of explanations about life and let us get back to my exercise routine. I spent so much time performing weight lifting. I lifted the metal bars and it enabled me to have the stamina to work at my career job.

Suddenly, I heard my stomach groaning. Maybe if I toss some food to that stomach of mine, it will keep quiet.

Angrily, I yelled, "Shut up stomach! Let me concentrate."

My complimentary apology to my readers and audiences; please excuse my language, I couldn't cheat nature. Despite, I tried so hard.

I headed to my wardrobe to pick up the best outfit for my work routine.

However, I had a bad habit within me. I always carry my magnifier with me wherever I go. I turned the lights on and picked up my deep brown–striped dressed shirt. I love to dress up for work and it kept me ready for business during the day. I specified my dressed outfit as first impression for business orientation. I brewed a cup of coffee which would wake me up for the whole day at work. I just did not have time to consume my cup of coffee. Yes indeed, I was living large at a high rise residential building. There was a huge balcony and patio at the top of the high rise building and a big swimming pool.

I extended my complimentary gesture to the great developers of the high-rise building.

The engineers, architects, & developers, "keep up the good work, I enjoy the views."

It was time for me to step out of my resident. However, I did not want to be late for work.

I stepped into the train station and took the express train to work. While I was on the train, I came across a young lady at her late twenties. She glanced at me and I wondered if I had something on my head or nose. I hope a pigeon wouldn't stain my head with its waste (dump).

Frequently, I touched my head while stepping out of my residence.

Frequently, I had the feeling that there were pigeons on the roof of the building. Purposely, the pigeons were trying to be creative towards my head. From my observation, it seemed as if the pigeons were studying each move I made at my place.

Cautiously, I wouldn't let those pigeons ruin my day when heading out from my residence, "Enough of my speculation, and let us go back to the beautiful young lady on the train." I glanced at my suit and dressed shirt. My magnifier didn't show me any stain on my suit.

I thought, "Wow! She must be interested in me." And I really admired her gesture. She was petite and beautiful. she smiled at me and I had to return her complimentary gesture with respect. She made a complimentary gesture towards my designer's suit. I referred to my whole apparel as 'the classics' of business.

My outfits were imported and were made from the finest material from the world. Definitely, my suits were tailored-made from the world. Creatively, I admired and loved the word 'quality' in the fashion life style of the business world.

I thought for a while, "Enough of my words of admirations toward my precious wardrobe."

Let us get back to the young beautiful lady.

I was blushing and I responded to her complimentary gesture.

The train made it to my final destination.

As I was about to head out of the train, I noticed she worked in one of the buildings of my job. I glanced at her face. I could see a glimpse of her eyes and lips.

For seconds, I extended some complimentary words of gestures within me.

I thought deeply and extended my gratitude to all the ladies.

Blushingly, I hailed, "Heavens! Gracious for this beauty! Can I get praised for this beautiful lady?"

She was so beautiful. Respectfully, we shook hands and introduced each other.

We exchanged complimentary business cards and she smiled.

She walked away and I headed my way to the office to start my work routine.

Suddenly, she texted me from her cell phone for lunch. Joyfully, I responded to her text-message.

We headed to the company's food big lounge. The company's food lounge was well equipped with enriched ingredients. The company's food lounge was bigger than I thought.

I ordered some healthy baked chicken with steamed rice and steamed broccoli. She ordered the same menu that I requested for lunch. I chatted with her about how the technology of the world had improved and changed the world.

We chatted about how the telecommunication system had advanced in the entire universe. We talked about high tech cell phones, touch screens, mp3, laptops, etc. She was very intelligent and funny.

Couple of times, we laughed and enjoyed the dish of the day.

She asked me what I was doing on Friday night. I told her I was not doing anything.

However, I told her that I was thinking of completing high tech projects at my place.

She smiled at me and I smiled back at her. I managed to make a dinner date with her after work hours. We planned on heading to the movies after work. She requested me to meet with her in fifteen minutes after work. I agreed with her happily. There was one thing I notice in the food lounge. The crowd was very quiet at the lounge room.

I looked around me and I noticed one thing, there were 'all eyes' on me. I realized my co-workers were laughing at me. They must be surprised to see me approach the young beautiful lady. Respectfully, she caught my attention and everything went well for the day.

One of my co-workers tossed a joke about me being a slacker.

They were surprised to see me handle everything well with the young beautiful lady.

Naturally, I was not perfect and I had so much to learn about life. I was relating to the dating, movie, theatre, and topic of the day. Don't get me wrong, these are beautiful ladies I love always.

I wanted to make time for these young beautiful ladies.

The problem was that I was so pre-occupied with my personal projects at work and home.

Success was my personal ambition. I was so busy taking care of some charity work for the community.

It was like getting married to my work routine and personal projects.

Enough of my speculation and let us get back to the young beautiful lady at the lounge room.

Lunch was over and we headed back to our work routines. I walked towards my office and one of my co-workers praised me.

A co-worker whispered, "Mr. Jacob, you did a great job with that young beautiful lady at lunch time."

I replied and thanked him.

Another co-worker walked towards me and said, "Don't blow this up, she's very beautiful."

It was almost time for my work routine to be over for the day. It was 3pm and I stepped out to wait for her on the first floor. She was going to meet me in 15 minutes on the first floor. I sat down on the visitor's complimentary seat on the first floor. I had ten more minutes for her to arrive on the first floor. I was feeling so hot and I was sweating.

I decided to step outside to get some fresh air. My mind was telling me not to step out of the building. Carelessly, I ignored my instinct. I stepped outside and I felt something dropped on my head.

I yelled angrily, "What was that thing that dropped on my head?

I took out my mini magnifier. I looked up to the top-roof of the high rise building of my job.

I saw a pigeon and the pigeon was shaking its buttocks toward me.

Angrily, I yelled at myself, "No! Not in my face...! No!

"Was I dreaming or what? Who sent this pigeon to ruin my date?"

Mercy! This can't be happening to me. I glanced at my magnifier and realized the pigeon was laughing at me. Repeatedly, I yelled angrily, "This is not funny . . . you, pigeon, you ruined my date."

I realized my suit was stained with the pigeon's waste. I glanced at my wrist watch and realized she was arriving in six minutes to get to me. She was heading down to the first floor.

Dear readers,

Can you all take a look at my designer's suit? There was **no—way** I could let her see me with a stain on my suit. Time was running out. The stupid pigeon ruined my date.

How I wished I could get my hands on that pigeon and give it serious smacking of life.

Respectfully, I called her from my cell phone and told her there was an emergency.

I apologized to her that I wouldn't be able to make it to the movie show and dinner.

I called the taxi driver at the park section and jumped in and drove off.

The taxi driver asked me, "What have you been feeding on, Bird's bubble gum or what . . . . ?"

For 20 seconds, I was speechless and I ignored the taxi driver's comment.

Disgracefully, I didn't have time for any bubble gum's joke and it wasn't funny.

That pigeon ruined my date and I couldn't wait to get my hands on that pigeon.

I thought angrily, "How I wished I could get my hands on that pigeon."

The taxi driver yelled politely, "Please, don't punch my face, I can't fight, and it has been a rough day for me too."

Again, the taxi driver yelled, "Check my driving tickets."

I kept quiet and ignored the taxis driver's comment.

To be continued . . . .

Vocabulary: A taxicab, also taxi or cab, is a type of vehicle for hire with a driver, used by a one passenger or small group of passengers often for a non-shared ride.

Thanks for Reading. My Appreciation!

BIOGRAPHY

Every experience and action in life creates an interesting story. However, the mind creates that space of element to be creative. And that enables me to write and direct stories in series. I would say art is one of the strongest forces in the world. However, interactive clement makes it more interesting (Phenomenon).

Creatively, it makes communication much easier for one to achieve. Art can take anyone anywhere they wish to go. Art has an irresistible effcct on most artists and writers: especially the talented ones who do not know why they have been given these creative skills. Art is not something that can be given up easily.

Humbly, I have elevated into writing, designing, drawing, directing stories, producing movies, and creating computer generated interactive images.

This new comedy and series' book I have written were designed for entertaining with a sense of humor.

Definitely, my new movie book creates illusion in every story as written. From the series, I produced this movie in sequences of how the animals interfere with the human nature in life (insects, etc).

Generously, I would like to extend my respect and gratitude to everyone. Thanks for reading my new movie book.

"Interactive element is phenomenon; it makes communication easier"
"Interactive clement is phenomenon and a good source of communication."
"Creative ideas come from the thought & mind, which improves the atmospheric condition of the environment."
*"It creates an interesting taste of knowledge (**Excitement/humor/Endurance/illusion**)."*
"Being famous and having fame in life is not easy. It's like asking for autographs. And one doesn't get noticed at first. We are all great."
"Peaceful mind creates peaceful thoughts, adequate space too."
"We learn through great life experience, it makes us stronger in person and in nature, and then we cherish gold at the end."
"We are all creative. We have creative minds. It doesn't matter who you are. You have creative mind stored within you." **Author / Producer: Damola Taiwo**

About My New book:

My new book tells us how the animal affects one's nature (atmospheric condition). These animals are the termites, insects, bees, ants, spiders, etc. The actual name I used for my main character is known as **Baba Bose**. However, I decided to combine the words together and I added the letter '**G**' to the name to make it more unique. It's a native name if not changed or combined. It's a masculine name: **Baba**. Baba means '**father**' or a '**big man**' (Baba 0). **Bose** is a feminine name. For example: **Baba Bose** (The Father of 'Bose'). However, it varies on how it is used.

Babagbose's favorite dessert is Roasted plantains with Roasted peanuts (Translation: e pa :nuts)

Vocabulary Used In This Movie Book:

Phenomenon Something that seems out of the ordinary and excites people's interest and curiosity

Speculation
A conclusion, opinion, or theory, based on an incomplete fact or information

Spank
To slap on the surface with a flat object or with the open hand, as for punishment. To move briskly or spiritedly. A slap on the surface.

Spanking
Exceptional of its kind; remarkable: unusual / worthy of notice. Swift and vigorous: a spanking pace. Brisk and fresh: a spanking breeze. Used as an intensive: a spanking clean shirt. An achieved total of slaps on the surface.

Smacking
Brisk; vigorous; spanking: a smacking breeze.

Blushing To turn red in the face because of emotion, especially embarrassment, shame, modesty, or pleasure.

Flirt Somebody who behaves in a playfully alluring way or in an interesting way.

Animals
Animals depend on other organisms for food.
All animals are heterotrophy, which means they cannot produce their own foods. Instead, they must consume plants and other organisms as a way to obtain the carbon and energy they need to live.

Mosquitoe(s) A fly with mouth section that is adapted to biting and piercing humans and other invertebrates.

Horns: A hard substance that covers an animal's horns (sharp), which contains mainly of a tough protein keratin

Goats: Naturally, most goats have multiple horns in different shapes and sizes depending on the Breed

N.B: Some content of this Movie book may not be suitable for underage. Please, read responsibly.

ABOUT THE CHARACTER: Babagbose has that characteristics of having pride and appreciation towards whatever comes around him. Although, he went through so many consequences and that made him stronger to withstand what was around him. However, he wasn't able to face everything that he encountered. He was getting familiar with the creative environment.

HIGH DEFINITION ANIMATION COMING SOON!

Printed in the United States
By Bookmasters